IF YOU ARE STRUGGLING

One Woman's Journey through Bi Polar Disorder, Trauma, and a Split Personality

BEVERLY ANN NEEDHAM

Copyright © 2019 by Beverly Ann Needham.

ISBN   Softcover   978-1-950580-20-0
         Ebook   978-1-950580-44-6

All rights reserved. No part of this book may be reproduced or transmitted in any form or by any means, electronic or mechanical, including photocopying, recording, or by any information storage and retrieval system without express written permission from the author, except in the case of brief quotations embodied in critical reviews and certain other non-commercial uses permitted by copyright law.

Printed in the United States of America.

To order additional copies of this book, contact:
Bookwhip
1-855-339-3589
https://www.bookwhip.com

Praise for If You Are Struggling

One woman with a Crystal Meth addiction said, "Now that I've read Beverly's story, I feel there's hope for someone like me—If Beverly can get through what she got through, then maybe I can too," And she recovered.

"This is an amazing book for people who have hit rock bottom. It's not a text book where somebody says, 'These are the statistics and if you do this, then such and such will happen.' No, this is from someone who went through it."
—Mrs. Dzebzenko

"Thank you for writing this book. Now I'm not alone. I can understand my own life better and share my story with more courage."
—Pvt. Ben Sullivan, U.S. Army, former foster child

"Thank you very, very much for helping me to not feel alone."
—Pat Bend, a New York man, diagnosed with bipolar

"This is a frank, eye-opening book and the best book on bi-polar disorder that I have ever seen. It will help a lot of people."
—Jeanette Hill, California High School Teacher

"Excellent book, very insightful."
—Bud Andreasen, Marriage and Family Therapist

"I rarely read, but this is an exception. I stayed up all night to finish this book. It puts into words what all of us feel, but none of us know how to express."
—Gil Dans (trucker and mason)

CONTENTS

Forward vii
Introduction ix
Prologue: My Ferris Wheel Ride xi

Chapter 1. No Two Snowflakes Are Alike............................1
Chapter 2. Like A Teddy Bear Is To A Child 15
    Introduction 15

    OUTLINE A: My Multiple Personalities & Their
    Helpful Counterparts 18
    "Little b" (Isolation Versus Reaching Out)......................20
    "Liz" (Hate Versus Love)..28
    "Pacita" (Defensive Versus Negotiating).......................32
    "Cara" (Frozen Feelings Versus Alive Emotions) 36
    "Keiko" (Judgment Versus Mercy)................................39
    "Lisa" (Drivenness Versus Kindness)............................42
    "Tammy" (Perfectionism Versus Reaching
    Your Own Goals)..45
    "Rebeccah" (Seeking Love Versus Giving Love)............52
    "Leah" (Vanity Versus Being Yourself) 56
    "Jamie" (Offensive Versus Forgiving).............................59
    "Emily" (Loneliness Versus Reaching For
    Your Dreams) 64
    "The Eagle" (Acceptance and Comfort) 69

    OUTLINE B: A SIMPLE CREED 72

Chapter 3. The Old Gray Mare Just Ain't What
               She Used To Be 74
Chapter 4. A Shrink In The Rink...96

Chapter 5. Like A Bridge Over Troubled Waters 113
Chapter 6. Poisoned Birds And Bees 120
Chapter 7. Rain Makes The Flowers Grow 128
Chapter 8. The Sun Shining Through The Clouds 142

Epilogue: My Ferris Wheel Ride Is Over 149
Denouement 155
Afterward 161
Appendix 1: Poetic Life Sketch 163
Appendix 2: Factual Life Sketch 167
Appendix 4: Songs to Share 169
    Always a Dream 170
    I'll Love You As You Are 171
    I'll Never Forget You 172
    My Inspiration 173

Appendix 4: Questions for Book Clubs and Study Groups .. 175
Book References 177

FORWARD

By Beverly Ann Needham
January 2019

When I wrote the following story at the turn of the century, I was going through the hardest time of my life. My suicidal and violent tendencies had grown worse during the 13 years in which I was medicated for severe depression. At that time, my psychiatrist told me, with exasperation, "I have no recourse except to give you more medication. But I don't want to do that. That would almost knock you out, and you are already the most medicated, sincere patient I have."

That was 20 years ago. My heart feels heavy just to think about those days. However, as I went through those days, I wrote this book. Writing was a lifeline—a catharsis that kept me from losing my mind. By sharing what was happening in my life and how I felt about it, I found some relief.

I hope my story will be a lifeline of hope, validation, and understanding to others who are struggling.

In this 2nd edition of "If You Are Struggling," the eight chapters remain primarily in their original state—as they were written before the Spring of 1999—before I found significant healing for depression, bipolar disorder and a split personality.

INTRODUCTION
1999

This story is true. Beverly and her friends, relatives, and pets which are mentioned in this book are real persons or animals, although in some cases their names are changed. A few details are slightly modified for simplicity.

Persons mentioned in this book are as follows.
    Beverly Ann Needham, age 45*.
    Her husband, Gregory A. Needham, age 46.
    Tim and Samuel** twins, age 21.
    Eli**, age 19.
    Christy, age 18.
    Butterfly**, age 16.
    Phillip**, age 14.
    Matthew, (Matt), age 6.
    Family Practitioner: Dr. Chevy**.
    Psychiatrist: Dr. Williams**.
    Psychotherapists:
    Larry Mansell,
    Gary Golden,
    Cheri McDonald,
    and Patrick Poor.

* (All ages are the ages at 2/99, when the chapters of this book were first completed.)
**(A nickname.)
    All poems are written by Beverly Ann Needham.

NOT ALONE (6/11/99)
    "We read to know we're not alone."
    C. S. Lewis hit it home.
    To learn another shares my pain,
    Gives me faith and hope again.

PROLOGUE

My Ferris Wheel Ride

Dear struggling friend or interested person,

Ever since I was a little girl I have wanted to write a book. Finally, my desire has become irresistible. My writings cannot be appreciated by those who manage to stay happy most of the time and don't enjoy reading of sad things. But I write for people who find comfort in reading of sad things, for then they know they are not alone.

Lately my life has been a Ferris wheel ride, hovering at the top, where I am full of excitement, grand ideas (like writing a book all in one month), staying awake half the night working on irresistible projects, and donating my time to community service. Then I find myself at the bottom of the Ferris wheel with such anxiety, despair, and anguish, that I feel death would be a welcome relief. Problems appear blown out of proportion many times their size and my sense of judgment is impaired drastically. My Ferris wheel ride keeps taking me up and down at irregular speeds, cycling several times a day. I'm learning to recognize when I'm at the top of the Ferris wheel, and to check myself, decide to do less, dream less, reprioritize, and rest more. And when I'm at the bottom, I've had to learn many coping skills to keep myself and others alive. I dream of a day when I don't live with fatigue. I can't recall the last time I've had such a day. I've spent long hours in bed. I've felt as though my legs were made out of rubber. I've been weighed down with extreme, heavy, relentless fatigue.

I express myself in many ways. Writing is one. Sometimes I write when I want to scream, or die, or when I am so racked with anguish, that I can't bear it. Writing gives me a release, and sometimes turns my grief around.

HANGING ON (11/5/96)
Sometimes I want to sweep things off the shelf,
Crashing and breaking, expressing myself.
I hang on until I'm no longer blind.
I've ridden it out, for one more time.

EXHAUSTED (@3/97)
Exhausted to the bone,
Can't seem to fall asleep.
My mind just wants to scream,
My heart just wants to weep.

God knows I'm going crazy!
Noises give me stress.
My mind is racing wildly.
A pressure's in my chest.

I'm starting to feel crabby.
It's time to isolate.
Can I endure much longer?
I just must not lose faith.

CHAPTER 1

No Two Snowflakes Are Alike

BIPOLAR DISORDER (12/26/98)

When I first tried to write this chapter on bipolar disorder (formerly dubbed by the medical field as manic depressive disorder), I showed it to my psychiatrist, Dr. Williams. He said I was not qualified to write a medical explanation of bipolar disorder. Nevertheless, he corrected some of my mistakes, and encouraged me to continue writing in other ways.

Perhaps I lack medical training, but I do not lack experience. So I'll try again to write this chapter about manic depression. This time, from my heart.

DIARY ENTRY (1/4/99)

This week I received in the mail an essay on some 1953 shock treatments from a mental patient's standpoint. I didn't want to read it. My wounds from having a mind that doesn't work right are too sore for me to read about what could have happened to me had I been born earlier. But the essay was from a loved one, so I read it. And I hurt inside. The 1953 shock treatments were a very bad experience for him. I was glad he trusted in me enough to share.

I had seen this loved one throughout my life be judged by various family members who didn't understand him.

Some family members thought it was some sin that made him distressed or suicidal. They thought that a mentally ill mind was a mind swayed by the devil. It took me many years before I found out for myself what a good character this mentally ill person has. I recently began a correspondence with him and his caregivers, and found them to be some of the most compassionate and understanding people I have ever met.

Many people have been very kind to me concerning my bipolar disorder. The concern and compassion they give to me make my life easier. It balances out animosity from other people. My fourteen-year-old son Philip recently told me that his brothers and sisters would probably like me more if I didn't tell them about my psychotic symptoms. "As for that," he added, "Dad would probably like you more if you didn't tell him, too!" Yet Philip said he doesn't mind if I tell him about my psychotic moments. A few of his friends even find mental health problems very interesting. They are accepting that I have mental illness, and anxious to learn about it. I appreciate those few understanding and interested friends who I can talk to.

ALONE
I've got a little problem.
(It's actually very big).
It impacts sleep and strength and stress
And if I will to live.

I find most folks don't understand.
But I can't run away.
It weaves through every part of me,
In ways I cannot say.

DIARY ENTRY (1/4/99)

When I was diagnosed as bipolar, I felt lonesome for someone to talk to who would know from experience what it's like to have bipolar disorder. But the telephone number of the first person I heard of that had bipolar disorder was withheld from me. I was refused an opportunity to contact a possible source of comfort and support. And I was cautioned to be undisclosing about my sickness because of its stigma. I felt so alone. Intended or not I felt my personal value was lowered. But the pain from peer reactions is only a ripple in comparison to the devastating floods of despair that often flow from my brain. So far I'm a survivor of the illness. But I don't feel like cheering. So much has been lost as a result of my sickness. Yet so much had been gained, like increased compassion, and faith in God. I feel more sensitive to others suffering. I felt tender compassion when the hurricane, El Nino, recently brought the ocean several miles inland to where a school teacher lived with her family in Honduras. The last of her struggles to keep her family together ended with her infant torn out of her arms by the swirling flood. She floated on palm leaves and debris in the ocean for days, nourished by an occasional coconut that floated by. She prayed and sang hymns to keep her heart from giving up. I read in the newspaper about her rescue, and about her loss. And I cried. Her husband, her three children, and her relatives are dead. I sense a glimpse of her pain. I sense her loss of hope.

AMATUER DESCRIPTION OF BIPOLAR DISORDER

Now that I've shared some of my personal feelings, I defy my psychiatrist's recommendation and present my 'nonprofessional' explanation of bipolar disorder.

Bipolar disorder has a manic state and a depressed state. Here is a description of my manic state: I talk fast, change subjects fast, and get overly excited in happiness, and in anger. My excited emotions have more power than my brain's logic. I can't sleep normally either.

Here is a description of my depressed state: I condemn and accuse myself of deep badness. I feel people hate and condemn me. I feel despair. Suicidal urges become as common as a dusty breeze on a country road. I have often been too weak to get out of bed, even on Christmas morning. And too weak to open my eyes to read a book. (Unfortunately, my psychiatrist has diagnosed me as having rapid cycling, mixed state bipolar disorder. This means that my symptoms change rapidly, and I often have 'manic' symptoms and 'depressed' symptoms at the same time. This type of bipolar disorder is the hardest kind to treat.)

I have been told that my brain's "neurotransmitters" and my brain's "electrolytes" are mixed up. (My amateur view of a neurotransmitter is that it is a street when it comes to an intersection; and an electrolyte is the signal light indicating stop, go, or slow down.) Different types of depression are linked to different neurotransmitters and different medications affect different neurotransmitters. (Since my mind is not transparent, my family practitioner and my psychiatrist have experimented on me with more medicines than I can count to try to find which medicines will work for me—without much success.)

If You Are Struggling

Have you ever tried to eliminate stress when you have too much to do in too little time? How about when people you love add a little stress to your life when they have a few problems of their own? Maybe, like divorcing you to marry the computer, driving your new car off a cliff, washing the carpet with shortening, and coming down with acute appendicitis during your brother's wedding. (I won't say which one I made up.)

Lithium, Depakote, antidepressants, and other psychiatric drugs have been used to treat my bipolar disorder. Also psychotherapy has been used. My psychiatrist, while prescribing medicine, has supported psychotherapy. But do I see emotional stability and physical strength? Well, let's just say that I have had a poor response to treatment, I'm getting used to my lack of strength as a way of life and the threat of suicide continues. It seems I switch from despair to cheerful mania without outward provocation.

Although everyone experiences emotional pain, bipolar disorder seems to compound my ability to cope with my pain. I feel overwhelming stress and deep emptiness. I keep feeling "cut down" as a person instead of "built up". I misinterpret daily events by viewing them with fear and leeriness. I have a feeling that I must not stand up for myself. Negative situations make me feel hopeless, like I am cornered. My beliefs over what is true and what is false seem to be at war inside of me. Psychotherapy has at times helped me to cope with or work through pain. And sometimes psychiatric medicines have blocked out my pain and detoured suicide. Sometimes, all of a sudden, my manner of thinking changes from despairing to hopeful without any effort on my part. I have managed to confuse both myself and my psychiatrist with my unpredictable mood swings.

Sometimes a person with bipolar disorder experiences psychotic symptoms such as hallucinations and delusions. Hospitalization is required for the individual who is suicidal, self-injurious, or a threat to others. (1/4/99 update–When I first wrote this chapter, I was glad hallucinations had not been a part of my life. But that comfort was short-lived. As I now finish this chapter, I possess empathy, born of new experience, for people who occasionally have to ask, "Was that noise real, or was it in my head?")

My bipolar disorder makes it hard for me to be dependable. I feel energetic and happy one moment, and depressed and exhausted the next. I make promises one day, but lack the strength and will power to carry them out the next.

I've heard that no two snowflakes are alike. So it is with every individual person, including those with bipolar disorder. (My husband teased me after he read this paragraph. He re-quoted me by saying, "No two 'flakes' are alike". Because I know he loves me, I can take his teasing, and tease him right back.) Every person is important. (Even teasing husbands!)

Here are some profiles of persons who have been diagnosed with bipolar disorder. They are about people I know either personally or who I have learned about from mutual acquaintances. My intention is to illustrate that people with bipolar disorder have interests, diversities, and aspirations, not unlike the common population.

Again, my doctor indicated that I was not qualified to provide medical profiles. "Many patients are misdiagnosed," he said, "and the profiles may be inaccurate due to your lack of training." True, my training is not 'medical', it is of the heart.

The following profiles were compiled by myself between 1997 and 1998.

PROFILE #1
ANONYMOUS MALE

Age-18. Interests-CB radios and dune buggies.

Moody was diagnosed in a mental hospital by a staff doctor when he was of Jr. High age. He had been admitted for violence, mood swings, and for being 'out of control'.

Lithium and Depakote were prescribed. Moody resists taking medication. Moody has gone in and out of Juvenile Hall in relation to whether or not he is taking his medication.

Moody does not like talking about his bipolar disorder.

PROFILE #2
WEALTHY ANONYMOUS WOMAN

Age-Senior citizen. Interests-Physical fitness, walking, the beach, socials, showing kindness to people, nice clothes, and family.

When her husband died, she fell apart emotionally. She was diagnosed bipolar and required an around the clock nurse to help with medicine and supervision to keep her from wandering off.

She became disoriented in her established home. But her eventual placement in a Senior Citizen's Home led to further disorientation and dismay.

PROFILE#3
ADORABLE ANONYMOUS.

Age-6 years old. Interests-Normal little girl interests from scholastics to mud pies.

A few years ago Adorable had a lengthy display of severe screaming, crying, destructiveness, fits of anger, and of being a danger to herself and others. She spent several weeks in a mental hospital for observation and treatment. The doctors finally conceded upon bipolar disorder as the diagnosis. They experimented with different amounts of Depakote until they found what worked best for her. Her parents went through counseling. They learned the importance of a strict regime for their daughter, and made changes in their own lives. A pending divorce was offset as the parents faced the crisis together.

Adorable is now a wonderfully delightful, attentive, and happy child. Her parents deserve credit for giving their daughter support, and for hanging in there, for it wasn't easy.

PROFILE #4
ANONYMOUS MOTHER.

Age-Middle aged.

Diagnosed bipolar, Angry will not take her prescribed medicine. Instead she has turned to illegal drugs. She has lost custody of her children. She manically complains to her family about her problems. Some family members screen out her phone calls to preserve their own sanity.

PROFILE #5
ANONYMOUS WOMAN

Age-Middle Aged.

Carefree was professionally diagnosed as having bipolar disorder and given lithium, which she has since discontinued because she feels no more need for it.

Perhaps the most extreme example of her mind working improperly was when she went on a shopping spree following her husband's death. She spent over $5,000 on clothing for herself in one day. When she came home from shopping, she was shocked to realize how much she had bought. She took everything back.

Carefree does not like to disclose her bipolar disorder.

PROFILE #6
TROUBLED

Age-Middle aged. Interests-Animals.

Troubled is weary of holding onto a difficult, mistrustful life. She avoids doctors and counseling. She is afraid of people who want to help her. She feels too hopeless and frustrated to give any credence to what learning about bipolar disorder could do for her. She is trying to keep her daughter in her custody and trying to resist suicidal desires and extremely deep hopelessness. She hurts herself physically. Encouragement to receive counseling is met with suspicion.

PROFILE #7
BEV (ME).

Age-44 (in 1997). Interests-Family, nature, writing, music, sports, and helping people.

"I was diagnosed as having bipolar disorder by my psychiatrist, Dr. Williams, a few years ago. Before that I was treated by my family practitioner for eight years for depression. Perhaps I was hard to diagnose because I kept my problems and my symptoms to myself.

I am presently taking lithium and an anti-depressant, two medicines for psychosis and mania, and thyroid and sleep medicines. Still, I live daily with fatigue. Manic stages and depressed stages switch back and forth without any stage of normalcy in between. Problems with alters (a type of multiple personality), self-abasement, and mistrust seem to come during my depressed stages.

"I'm comforted mainly by my writing, and by One who knows and understands what I'm going through."

PROFILE #8
ANONYMOUS TEEN

Age-14. Interests-Art, animals, country music, and helping others.

In the months following a violent assault by a serial rapist and murderer, Resilient suffered from insomnia and despair. With her mother's encouragement, she sought relief from a psychiatrist. She presented psychotic symptoms and suicidal thoughts. She was diagnosed as having bipolar disorder. Soon after, she felt better, slept better, and discontinued her medicine. A year later, she threatened to hurt her little brother, and a few hours later attacked her mother by pulling her off her chair by her hair and dragging her to the ground. Resilient was admitted into a psychiatric hospital that night. After her release, she was stable, and the hospital psychiatrist suggested that her former diagnosis of bipolar disorder was a misdiagnosis—his opinion differing from that of the other psychiatrist. Resilient commented, "I learned to never attack my mother again, or I'd get thrown in the mental hospital."*

*(2019 I later learned that Resilient never took psych medicine for bipolar or anything else. She hid the pills in her cheek & spit

them out when no one was looking. "I didn't want to be like my mother who was on psych meds," she said. So her recovery had nothing to do with the drugs.)

PROFILE #9
ANONYMOUS GIRL

Age-11. Interests-Animals, friends, and helping people.

Friendly was diagnosed bipolar when she had an episode of suicide attempts. She spent many months living in a psychiatric facility. Presently she has been allowed to live at home, but commutes to the hospital school every day. She takes Depakote, which has made a significant improvement. She tries to follow her doctors' and counselors' guidance in order to avoid a return trip to live in the hospital. Improved relations with her mother have enhanced her success. Her father has not been a part of her life since earlier years.

PROFILE #10
HELPFUL

Age-Middle aged. Interests-Family, helping others, and creative pursuits.

Helpful spent a few years in bed without a diagnosis. She'd collapse if she got up to do something. She couldn't lift her head, or talk. In time she was diagnosed bipolar but she was unresponsive to medication. The main thing that worked for Helpful was for her to pace herself and not overdo. She has a very large family. She and her husband received counseling to help them work together better.

She appreciates her family for hanging in there. These last few years she's spent a month here, and a month there, helping a sick relative or a family member with a new baby. She's given lectures, traveled, and offered phone support to others suffering from bipolar disorder. In her spare time she creates and markets scrap books and children's journals. She stays healthy by resting when she gets tired. Medication has not been very effective, although she has tried many kinds.

PROFILE #11
ALICE

Age-Mid twenties. Interests-Hiking and friends.

I met Alice a few years ago in a pharmacy when I noticed she was picking up Lithium like me. I had barely begun taking Lithium and knew almost no one with bipolar disorder. Alice told me that Lithium keeps her out of the psychiatric hospital, yet she still can't live a normal life. She's learning to accept a limited ability for driving, employment, recreation, housework, etc. She takes one day at a time and relies on God for assistance.

COMPOSITE PROFILE #1
PAT, STEVE, AND AUSTIN

Ages-Mid twenties to senior citizens. Composite Interests: The ocean, family, travel, and geology.

These men suffered through a lot before being diagnosed as having bipolar disorder. Presently Lithium and anti-psychotic medications reduce their symptoms. Suicide attempts, psychosis, misdiagnoses, hospitalization, heavy and lengthy tranquilization, and old fashioned shock treatments make up some of their past experiences. Two of these men, unemployed, have depended on their family for support. At least one still suffers from depression. Yet these caring and sensitive men have rendered themselves helpful to family and friends. In addition, one has pursued a successful career as a geologist. He has created many life-size dinosaur replicas, some excellent scientific texts, and valuable research.

COMPOSITE PROFILE #2
THREE ANONYMOUS WOMEN

Ages-Middle aged to senior citizen.

These women were diagnosed bipolar after suffering through some very hard times emotionally. Lithium has helped one woman to live a normal life. Another woman continues to relapse intermittently. One woman, whose bipolar disorder is compounded with other diseases, has not yet responded to medication and is having prolonged difficulties.

DIARY ENTRY (1/12/99)

After typing these profiles into my computer I feel less self-centered. I view the remainder of my day in a more calm way. You see, yesterday I was so exhausted from a twelve hour work day that I cried myself to sleep at night. I lamented over not being able to do lots of things without collapsing in exhaustion and pain afterward. As today began, I found it nearly impossible just to get dressed. I even ate with my head down. So typing all these profiles has been an exertion. Yet I feel less angry and frustrated over my low strength than I did before, because I am not the only one who is struggling.

SIMPLE REPRIEVE (1/12/99)

Sometimes when my mind is ill,
I'm scared. I run away.
No strength to move at other times,
Distressed, I simply lay.

But what I like the best,
Be there strength, or none at all,
Is when my thoughts are calm,
With no despair at all.

SURVIVING (2/11/96)

I feel overwhelmed.
Life isn't right.
I'll turn to you, God,
So I won't feel uptight.

My feelings are awful.
No answers are near.
I'll lean on thy sight,
For mine is unclear.

CHAPTER 2

Like A Teddy Bear Is To A Child

INTRODUCTION

When I was a small child I had a pastel-colored, stuffed elephant. I pretended it protected me at night. By the time I was twelve I'd begun having nightmares. My parents would comfort me when I'd call out. When I was sixteen, I told my counselor at summer camp that I was afraid of Satan at night. She calmed me and encouraged me to have faith in God's protection. Sixteen years later, I had a breakdown. Previously unexpressed painful feelings flooded my mind. My nightmares and fears resurfaced. One night, upon retiring with my husband, I felt an ominous presence trying to come between us. Whether an illusion or some real, dark power, it was the most evil influence I've ever felt before or since. Silent prayer gave me an idea to cling to, that I'd lose my despair by focusing on someone other than myself. Unselfish thoughts toward my husband, and all the faith in God I could muster, helped me endure until the despair left.

I named this chapter "Like a Teddy Bear is to a Child", because when someone is scared, and they receive comfort, it's like a child snuggling up to a stuffed animal. I recently found a little blue stuffed elephant in a shop, like the one I had as a child, and I couldn't resist buying it. I seem to sleep better at night when it's nearby, to squeeze against my heart. I pretend it's absorbing all my pain.

My daughters used to play house with an imaginary friend, "Mr. Nobody". They would hear his imaginary knock at the door and let him in. I too have imaginary friends, and foes. Seven psychiatrists and psychologists have suggested I have multiple personality disorder. I thought that a person who had multiple personalities had no memory of the times they were the multiples. But I have memory of the behavior of my multiple personalities or of my "alters" as my psychiatrist calls them. Beginning in my teens and continuing into my forties now, I remember sudden impulses and sudden unreasonable ideas playing havoc with my otherwise good mind. My alters have given me mixed up or immature perceptions of myself and others.

This chapter shares how I've coped with having alters, or multiple personalities. I have privately named them and invented healthy counterparts for them. Each alter and its counterpart have the same name, but they represent opposite sides of the same trait. In my mind and in my writing I speak to these parts of myself. I nurture the good traits and flee from the bad.

DISCOVERING FRIENDS I HAVE INSIDE OF ME (9/17/97)
>One day I wrote a letter
>To the Bev back in the past.
>It seemed I felt her answer
>As I wrote her feelings back.
>
>One by one eleven parts
>Emerged from inside me.
>At first these parts seemed harmful,
>But I nursed them tenderly.

Back and forth between these parts
I'm juggled like a pin.
I work so hard to stop the hate
And bring the sweet love in.

At first when I disowned them,
My doctor was the one,
Who taught that they were parts of me,
And through love must be won.

He said I must have splintered
In days so long ago.
"Sequestered parts", he called them.
And I must make them whole.

These parts have often helped me
Like when my mind gets ill.
I write them for their insights
And old wounds start to heal.

OUTLINE A
My Multiple Personalities & Their Helpful Counterparts

Following is a brief sketch of my multiple personalities or 'alters' and their healthy counterparts as I perceived them in 1996.

LITTLE B
Alter-A child, alienated, afraid to trust anyone.
Counterpart-I try to reach out, forgive, trust, and love.

LIZ
Alter-Hateful, revengeful, suicidal, no trust or faith in anyone.
Counterpart-I try to be compassionate and assertive in standing up for my beliefs.

PACITA
Alter-Defiled, helpless, mistrustful, accusing, rageful, suicidal.
Counterpart-Shows respect, kindness, and is nick-named 'peaceful negotiator'.

CARA
Alter-Ashamed to feel pain, fatigue, anger, etc. Disclaims her feelings.
Counterpart-I accept my emotions compassionately, unburdened by guilt over having painful feelings.

KEIKO
Alter-Judges, feels judged, condemned, criticized, and defensive.
Counterpart-I try to have mercy for myself and others.

LISA

Alter-'Driven', denied freedom to be herself, fearful of annihilation for 'badness'.

Counterpart-Ceases 'running' to stop and 'smell the daisies'.

TAMMY

Alter-Perfectionistic, according to other people's standards. Fears their condemnation.

Counterpart-Lives up to her standards, not other people's unrealistic expectations.

REBECCAH

Alter-Needy for love, yet doubts love when it is there.

Counterpart-I try to rise above loneliness and pain through loving others.

LEAH

Alter-Feelings of superiority and pride alternate with feelings of being condemned and mocked.

Counterpart-I don't seek to impress others, I simply try to be my genuine self.

JAMIE

Alter-Believes she must not disagree with others nor have anger, yet she erupts into sudden violence followed by suicidalness.

Counterpart-I try to express and accept differences fearlessly.

EMILY

Alter-A child denied freedom to be herself.

Counterpart-I reach for my dreams.

"Little b"
(Isolation Versus Reaching Out)

In December 1995, after being released from a brief stay in a psychiatric hospital, I began searching for answers as to why I wanted to die and why I struggled so hard to relate to others. I read "Men Are From Mars and Women Are From Venus" by Dr. John Gray. In Dr. Gray's book was a sample letter for communicating one's feelings. The sample letter had open-ended starters such as "I feel sad (or frightened, or angry, etc.) because. . . ." I enjoyed writing my feelings in these letters. I then read "The Path to Wholeness" by Susan Tuttle which is about recovering from sexual abuse. Susan Tuttle suggested writing to a part of oneself that was lost long ago in childhood. So I wrote to this distant child several times. I loved her. She was insecure and wary. I named her "beverly", or "Little b", perhaps because I wrote my name with a little "b" when I was first learning to write letters.

> LITTLE B SHARES WITH BEVERLY (12/27/95)
> I'm scared I'll do something wrong
> In a grownup's eyes.
> I will be rejected
> As their love for me just dies.
>
> I'm fearful that my friends will learn
> About my badness, too.
> I fear that they'll reject me,
> But I've found a friend in you.

I told a friend about my efforts to help "Little b" and of how frightened "Little b" was of others. My friend reacted with shock. She reprimanded me for writing such letters and told me it was of the devil. Feeling chastised and insecure, I followed her advice. I stopped writing Little b that day, somewhat relieved to turn my back on something I didn't understand, and which held so much pain. But I couldn't forget Little b forever. In March 1996 I started writing to Little b again.

DIARY ENTRY (3/96)

Little b-I just want someone around who doesn't act as though they don't see me. It hurts to not be noticed. I'm real sad. I'm scared and alone. Will you please help me? I want to be loved. I want to have a friend.

Bev-Dear b, What kind of person would you trust?

Little b-I trust someone who listens to me.

During the rainy days of March, I had many conversations with Little b. I found out that she lived in a cold, large house with little furniture, and endless empty rooms into which she would retreat. The house had no windows and no lights. Little b had lived there for many years alone.

BEVERLY'S SADNESS (4/1/96)
Love's the sweetest thing
I could write of.
I crave it. I thirst it.
Yet I've not even grub.

Totally alone
In this big house of mine.
No people. No furnishings.
Not even sunshine.

> I know there's a sun,
> And beauty somewhere.
> I know there is love,
> For my heart can care.
>
> Being alone
> Is the worst thing I know.
> As deep as my love,
> My sadness does flow.

Communicating with Little b was challenging, for she was quick to mistrust me. If I went too many days without writing to her, or if I ignored her pain, she would retreat from me. When I was extremely happy, she would retreat. She thought the sorrow she bore was being carelessly overlooked. Once, during a cozy moment with a book, I begged her to join my pleasure. But she would not share my joy. It seemed she needed me to acknowledge and share her sorrow. Once, as I stood on a hill, enjoying a breath-taking view of the Coral Red Sand Dunes in Southern Utah, I begged her to join my ecstasy, but she would not. Her pain was too great. And I was oblivious to her pain.

BATHE ME IN SADNESS (2/17/96)

> Bathe me in sadness.
> Fill the whole sea.
> God help me bear it.
> I'm so unhappy.
>
> With cut open heart,
> Give help! I implore.
> Make my heart bigger
> To bear what's in store.

> I'm hurting all over.
> What can I do?
> "For each tear that's shed,
> I'll give love to you."

Once, when Little b was offended by my insensitivity, she seemed to angrily turn into Liz, as in the following dialogue.

DIARY ENTRY (5/28/96)

Bev-Little b, I hear your cry far away inside my past. I'd like to open up and feel your pain and earn your trust and listen to you, but I'm numb.

Little b-I feel grown up now, as if I am Liz, and I want nothing to do with you in the way of trust.

Sometimes I went for days without being able to communicate with Little b. Yet I couldn't give up on Little b. She was only a child. I decided to try to reach her with a story. I made up a story for her about a little lost lamb whose name was "Little b".

THE LITTLE LOST LAMB

Once a lovely and precious lamb named Little b lived in a flock of sheep. One day Little b got separated from the flock. No one noticed she was gone, except the shepherd. He left the flock to look for her. He climbed the mountains to the South, to the East, and to the West. Up and down steep inclines he trekked, searching, listening, and calling. After many days the shepherd found Little b near a steep crevice. She had forgotten him and the flock since she had been gone for so long. The shepherd realized that winning her trust would be harder than finding her. For many days the shepherd kept his distance. After Little b began trusting him a small bit, they began walking together, the breeze on their backs, enjoying the sunset from the mountaintop. The shepherd listened to Little b's excitement over deer, insects, and flowers. Each night Little b slept in a cold, dark, deep cave. She would not sleep on the soft cushion of leaves that the shepherd made for her at the cave's entrance, where he kept watch. Then one night, after awakening from a terrible dream, Little b called out to the shepherd from the depths of the cave. The shepherd answered. His voice calmed her. The rest of that night Little b slept on the soft leaves at the cave's entrance, where the shepherd kept his watch.

Once the shepherd asked Little b if he could carry her back to the flock, but Little b said: "No.". . . .

(During the weeks in which I wrote The Little Lost Lamb I was in therapy with my psychiatrist. I told him Little b was not a part of me, but he said she was, that I just needed to accept that fact. So I longed for the feeling that she was a part of me. Whenever I asked her to come into my heart, she would not. Then one morning, I awoke very early, feeling unusually peaceful and calm. I wrote to Little b in my journal and we exchanged "I love yous". Little b thanked me for sharing her sadness. Then Little b asked me to finish the story.)

DIARY ENTRY (Spring 1996)

Bev-Would you like me to finish the Little Lost Lamb Story?

Little b-"Yes . . . but not in your room. Come on the hill with the clearing at the top-you know where I mean."

(I'd been there before. I left quickly. Bringing my diary, but forgetting the protection of my hiking boots, I started the climb clad in tennis shoes. The grasses were unusually tall and the trail was gone. Terrified of rattlesnakes, I hiked warily to the top, after which I let my

guard down. So happy to finally reach the top, without looking down, I stepped over a huge coiled snake without seeing it until it was under me. Frightened and unnerved, I went on to a serene and beautiful hilltop with golden, waving grass, two bushy trees, a soft breeze, and flowers. I sat down near one of the trees. I sang some of my favorite songs. Then I continued writing my story, with Little b's help.)

DIARY ENTRY ON THE HILL (Spring 1996)

Bev-After the nightmare, the lamb trusted the shepherd. Little b, how did you let him know you trusted him?

Little b-I simply jumped into his arms when I awoke in the morning, the same way your small son jumps into yours. Everywhere we went, if I wanted, he carried me. He told me you would help me go back to the flock when I was ready.

Bev-Little b, I was really scared to come here, but I hoped you would come into my heart here on this mountain. Yet now, the humming bugs sound like rattlesnakes rattling. Spiders, and strange sounds frighten me. Even the birds are beginning to frighten me. And thoughts of stepping over that huge snake still scare me. Do you know what I'd like to do?

Little b-You'd like to let me come inside you?

Bev-Yes . . . (But somehow I held back from believing she was a part of me.)

Little b-I don't care if you're scared. I care if you 'feel'. I need to go inside you, for as a child, I'm not safe alone with all my confusion and with feelings I can't understand that condemn me and hurt me.

I felt Little b say she'd come inside me in a prayer, and I did pray. And I stayed longer on the hill. But I still felt we were separate.

Soon I began to roast under the climbing sun. I feared I might faint from sun stroke, and nobody knew where I was. So I crawled under the bushy tree for shade. There had been some kind of animal scurrying about in the dry leaves under the tree. I had been listening to it for a long time. "Simply a squirrel or some other harmless animal," I reasoned. But as I crouched in the shade of the bushy tree, with my eyes not yet adjusted to the dark, my supposed furry friend did not scurry away. I listened to it approach me, but I couldn't see it. The moment 'slithering snake' entered my mind, I shot out from under the tree. I ran down the hill, making as much noise as possible to scare off any remaining snakes.

In my car, sometime later, I was happy that I had showed Little b that I cared. But I felt disappointed that I still felt separate from her. This time my silent prayer was very simple and sincere. "Please God, let Little b be one with me", and I felt an answer in my heart: *She already is*. I immediately knew God's answer was true, and I was very happy! I experienced no outward change. Yet in my heart I felt a peaceful, trusting, loving presence, and my acceptance of it.

Since that day, if I draw on the Little b part of me, I am able to be more open and trusting. One example was when I was frightened to see a new therapist. Relying on the Little b part of me calmed me down and helped me to be sincere and open, thus facilitating a beneficial therapy session. This simple, loving part of me helps me be genuine and to take down the fronts I put up.

Still sensitive and vulnerable to hurt, at times this childlike part of me still retreats. Yet if I seek Little b's true qualities, I am quiet, honest, open, and relaxed. I let myself feel sadness freely, which is healing.

HIDDEN SADNESS (2/21/96)

I wrote about sadness,
Then threw it away,
When I read my words
The following day.

A chapter unopened,
Or closed from the start.
I can't yet express it—
The pain in my heart.

So I'll cry when I hear
A beautiful song.
I'll cry when I realize
I'm guiltless, not wrong.

I'll remember each prayer
Brings me closer to see
I'm not a bad person.
I've compassion for me.

LITTLE B (12/2/96)

B denies not feelings.
"To accept hurt is O.K."
And with the hurt, she forgives,
In a frank and patient way.

As a Teddy Bear is to a child, so Little b is to me. Just thinking of her sincere and open way calms me and helps me face frightening situations with humility. Accepting sadness, and then giving love, helps me forget my pain.

"Liz"
(Hate Versus Love)

I recall sitting in my psychiatrist's office during a long 'bout with suicidal thoughts. I described a character whom I had named Liz, as one who hated me and wanted to destroy me. She hated others too, and lashed out at them.

DIARY ENTRY (3/31/96)

Beverly–There is no hope for Liz to ever be good. Definitely she should be destroyed. She's a liar, denies sadness, pain, and my standing up for myself. She hates others for walking on her, rejecting her, and for being untrustworthy towards her. She hates herself as well.

DIARY ENTRY (1996)

Liz-I used to believe I should be destroyed. I hated others fiercely. I was past feeling pain for being rejected. I pre-conditioned myself to do specific harmful things to myself and others at the first provocation. Beverly took precautions to avoid letting my rage and badness hurt her.

I thought Liz was outside of me, but my psychiatrist told me Liz was a part of me. He said she only acted the way she did because she was like a caged animal, poked at with sticks. She needed my compassion and understanding. "But how do I get her to stop being so hateful?" I asked. He replied, "Love her". So I did, and the Little b inside of me helped by giving unconditional and fearless love to Liz. I started to regard Liz as a part of myself.

DIARY ENTRY (4/12/96)

One day I went to a beautiful place of worship. It was very quiet there and I was alone with my thoughts and desires. As I walked from one room to the next, I saw a painting that appeared to represent Liz. It was a woman whom some may have considered awful. She had several husbands, or lovers, and lived many lies. She was at a well in the painting, giving Jesus a drink. Jesus' love and hope for her seemed to transform her right before my eyes into a new being. It seemed that there at the well, Liz was purified and healed of the hurt and pain that made her hate and lie. With her fresh start emerged a strength of character, and a leadership, and a wisdom that surpassed that of my other parts.

Having improved character traits in Liz, I entered a new era of less suicidal feelings, less helplessness, and more control over my life. For instance, I resisted submitting to the disrespect of grown children still living at home, and helped them move out. Then, while vacationing with seven small children, (ours' and our neighbors'), I called on the firmness and stubbornness of Liz to whip them into line when needed, yet I did so with kindness and respect.

INNER STRENGTH (@1996)
Liz is my friend.
She helps me be strong.
She lives in my heart.
She holds her ground long.

She will take the lead
Although it be rough.
She moved out the twins
Because she was tough.

> She kindly sets limits,
> Like on her last trip.
> With 3 extra kids,
> She used a firm lip.
>
> Greg was so proud.
> A tight ship was run.
> Without Liz's firmness
> It couldn't be done.

The following poems sum up the differences between the two sides of Liz.

LIZ (4/1/96)

> Liz, puffed in pride,
> And needing no one.
> She'll tear you down
> In the name of her fun.
>
> Can we convince her
> That she is not dirt?
> Understanding reveals—
> More than pride, she has hurt.

WORTH THE EFFORT (1996)

> It takes effort to win Liz
> From her awful state.
> I keep giving love,
> When she just gives hate.
>
> I've tried hard to stop
> Her cruel striking out,
> Her self debasement,
> Her uncontrolled shout.

If You Are Struggling

Little b's been brave,
Encouraging, and kind,
Dissolving all the pain
In Liz's heart and mind.

And Liz now leads the way
With patient, loving, care,
Encouragement, upliftment,
And sympathy so rare.

Her hatefulness resides
In days of long ago,
For efforts filled with love,
Have made her friend, not foe.

When I find myself being the old Liz, I seek a way to humble and soften my heart. Often it helps to think of the tarnished woman at the well, who was touched by the Master. Freed from pain, Liz's hate and rage are replaced with love and compassion, for myself, and for others.

If the newer Liz were a child's Teddy Bear she would be sturdy and strong. A child would feel protected with this bear. If Liz Bear got lost, the child would feel lost too.

"Pacita"
(Defensive Versus Negotiating)

My meeting of Pacita on April 22, 1996 is told as follows by Pacita and Beverly.

Pacita-When Beverly discovered me on a trip away from home she found out I felt angry, mistrustful, deceived, and taken advantage of. She tried to tell me that the world is not as bad as I pictured it. I didn't believe her. Mistrust filled up every part of me. She spoke of how beautiful the world was, and of loving, kind-heartedness, but I mocked her. It was all a trick. I was hardened, and not about to stick my neck out to trust. Then she played a cassette tape for me of children singing songs about good homes, good men, security, and trust. I couldn't help but listen. Gradually, the tender songs softened my heart. Their messages of leaders you could trust, of children enveloped in love and safety, and of families full of joy, opened a new side of my heart. I wanted to experience what the songs depicted. The peace, the trust, the purposefulness, and the joy, if I dared hope for it.

Beverly-On my way home, after discovering my new friend, I named her "Pacita" because "Paz" means "peace" in Spanish and I thought "ita" meant "little one" in Spanish, thus meaning: "little peacemaker". I later learned it did not translate as such, but Pacita liked her name anyway.

Since adolescence, I feared to trust close relationships.

My fear of hurt and rejection influenced my efforts to work out problems with others. I was often leery because I doubted their motives. Without trust in people, and at the same time, losing trust in prescribed medicine, I spiraled downward.

HATE (9/25/95)
    Hate?
    I hate!

    You bet I hate!
    I'm full of vengeance, too!

    To kill myself I crave the most
    When pain is caused by you!

    Stand up for myself?
    No. I mutely submit.
    I try to hold pain in.
    But it just doesn't fit!

    I'm hurt and confused.
    I know not where to turn
    To make meaning of this.
    But for peace I do yearn.

DIARY ENTRY (1997)

While discussing family rules with my husband Greg, a helpless, mistrustful, cornered feeling emerged repeatedly. Suicidal impulses necessitated that I withdraw from our conversations. I perceived that I felt old Pacita's mistrust. I searched inside myself for kindness and patience with my husband. Soon I was able to return to our discussions with good will.

    One evening I relapsed when Greg simply spoke his opinion. Greg and I could both see the sudden change that overcame me. Before I could breathe out one word, Greg saw it in my face. I felt it. The powerlessness, mistrust, hate, and rage. I hated feeling that way so much I wanted to die. This time I bit my tongue so as to not hurl out accusations that I sensed may be irrational. I was learning to catch myself. I went into an empty room and sat down and made up this poem. I realized Greg's opinion was not a threat to me. Although most of our marriage I thought myself wicked to have a different opinion from his, because I thought that's what my mother taught when she chastised me for sharing my problems with her. She wanted me to be happy without knowing I needed to accept sadness in order to feel the deepest joy. It was hard, but with Greg I started learning to respect and share my own opinion more.

SAYING "NO" (9/14/97)

I suffered much pain, so I built a defense.
Someone knocked it down, without recompense!
I know what I'll do. I'll forgive, and then,
With more faith and love, I'll build it again.

DIARY ENTRY (12/98)

I have two friends who love my children, but who don't know me well. One of them once called my husband and told him to divorce me or my whole family would go to hell. The other tried unsuccessfully to have my children taken away from me, saying I was a bad mother. This was because I shared my heartbreak with them over some of the problems my children and I were having. Ever since that time, we've been guarded around each another. A decade ago, I'd heard that if someone has hurt you, praying for that person helps you to feel better, and enables you to give up your grudge. Although I've prayed for these friends before, last night something happened inside of me when I prayed. I realized I must stop my side of the leery and guarded feelings. I decided to ask their forgiveness with a sincere heart. I knew that if they wouldn't forgive me, it would make no difference in my feelings of good will. After visiting each of these two friends today, I felt complete forgiveness and pure love toward each of them. One friend forgave me. The other did not. But as she spoke to express her feelings of hurt, I looked into her eyes and tried to understand. God opened my eyes to see the intents of her heart, which were to protect and love and help my children. Her love for my children touched my heart deeply. In her heart I saw a beauty and a goodness that I've never seen before. My mistrust and fear of her were replaced with peace in my own heart. I had forgiven. I harbored no ill will.

There is someone else—an old boyfriend—who I've been mad at for thirty years. I've gone back and forth between forgiving and hating him. My heart has changed toward him also, after a phone call where I told him what I wished I'd told him as a teen—to respect me. I think I shall never hate him again. Not because he changed, but because my nature seems to be more respectful of myself and more kind toward others. I wonder if trust could possibly become a strength instead of a weakness. I would be immeasurably grateful if I could trust more easily!

SMILING PACITA (5/5/96)
    Kind and smart Pacita,
    Ask her anything.
    She may not have the answer,
    But peacefulness she'll bring.

I have a sweet doll named Pacita. She has a constant smile. Were she a child's teddy bear, she'd bring faith. Faith in people. And hope. And goodwill for all.

"Cara"
(Frozen Feelings Versus Alive Emotions)

I first became aware of Cara in May 1996, after a family reunion. Unlike my husband's family, who talks somewhat openly about mental health problems, my family at the time was more reserved. I had recently been in the psychiatric hospital, and still couldn't hold my head up for most of the family reunion due to exhaustion. I wished I could talk to someone about my mental health challenges, but there seemed to be a complete avoidance of the subject of my health that night. Yet I had previously decided to think of my relatives instead of myself. So I gave love and thought of their needs, which helped me get through. Later that night, on the way home, I felt a very deep sadness inside of me. I let it fill my heart. I didn't deny it. I didn't feel guilty for being sad. And the new Cara emerged. Freed from feeling guilt for her feelings, the new Cara was able to feel pain without needing a reason, without needing an excuse.

    THE ILL CAT (5/96)
        A little ball, a little yarn,
        A little kitten at play.
        No one will do it any harm,
        Nor put poison in its way.

        No one slaps or pushes it,
        Nor breaks a tender bone.
        No one throws it in a pit,
        And leaves it all alone.

        No one yells and curses it,
        Nor takes away its toys.
        No striking out nor angry fit,
        For this cat will know joys.

I've faith that every suffering cry
Will someday turn to laughter.
I hope that kind and gentle ways
Will last forever after.

DIARY ENTRIES (5/4/96)

Beverly-Sometimes another's behavior or my thoughts of former happenings drain me of all my strength as if a plug were pulled, letting all my energy run out. It happens daily. I try to be firm, like Liz, and just go on. But it doesn't work. How do I find where I've gone wrong?

Cara-It is in your unacceptance that you're perturbed, tired, disappointed.

Beverly-When disappointed, tired, or frustrated a strong part of me like Liz can express it. Or a guilt-ridden part of me retreats, feeling shame for feeling disappointed, tired, frustrated, or any feeling of pain.

Cara-It's difficult for you because you can't always tell if you feel tired, perturbed, disappointed, angry, etc. I know you feel awful, even like dying when you suppress these emotions, but you don't perceive that you are even suppressing something.

Beverly-I feel very sad when you point that out to me.

Suppressing sadness I have done.
A million tears I have shunned.
Where is the place they hide?
It is very deep inside.

I sometimes feel as if I don't know "Sad". Although "Sad" can be a friend that shows me how to face things that will help me learn and grow. How can I accept sad feelings without suppressing them? What do I do?

Cara-That is a hard question. Pray. That will help.

MORE ABOUT CARA

It seemed I took to heart the well-meant but misleading phrase: "If you're living right, you're happy. If you're sad, it's because you're doing something wrong." If I was sad, I thought I was wicked. I denied sad, hurt, and angry feelings. I shunned the very emotions I needed to face in order to learn more sincerity, compassion, and faith.

> RELEASE FROM GUILT (1997)
> This morning I felt sad,
> And blamed myself of sin.
> Not knowing my offense,
> Nor where the sad began.
>
> And so I asked my God,
> "What have I done wrong?"
> "Nothing. It's pain you can't help.
> Just mourn, and then go on."

> RELEASE (2/27/99)
> Releasing pain is healing.
> It's hurt, which wrings my heart,
> Feels like a baby crying,
> Unconsoled from dawn to dark.
>
> Nothing I can do for it
> Can take away its pain.
> I hold it, watch it, feel its ache,
> Attentive, 'til tears wane.

If Cara were a Teddy Bear, she would cradle me when I walk through scary and new places, like through feelings I haven't faced before. Whether I feel bad because I have made a mistake or because other people think I have made a mistake when I haven't, Cara loves me the same.

"Keiko"
(Judgment Versus Mercy)

I discovered Keiko on Sunday, May 5, 1996. I didn't get out of our car when my husband parked it in our driveway after driving home from church. I leaned back and fell asleep. When I awoke, I was thinking, sadly, of how I felt people were critically judging me, and also of the discomfort I felt about my judgment of others. I became keenly aware of that judgmental part of me. And I named her "Keiko". For at least 30 years Keiko's characteristics had been with me. During this time, my diaries and journals gave countless accounts of my efforts to stop judging others and of my awareness of the prideful, better-than-thou attitude which I hated about myself. Whether I was judging others, or imagining that they were judging, despising, and condemning me, my peace was lost either way. I wrote the following nearly ten years before Keiko and my other parts were discovered. Its timing illustrates the longevity of some of my struggles.

   WHO AM I? (1988)
      Who am I,
      When standing all alone,
      Stripped of the pride
      That Satan briefly gives me?

      What are the thoughts,
      The feelings of my heart,
      When flowing freely
      On the wings of trust?

Can I trust me,
With motives chaste and kind?
Without the need
To answer to another?

Why do I fear
To speak, or be myself?
Am I not good?
On this hope can I cling?

Why do I make
Excuses to another?
Why do I feel
That I am in their judgment?

I'll seek to love,
And serve all that I meet.
Thoughts of them, a smile,
Will see me through.

DIARY ENTRIES (5/5/96)

Bev-Dear Keiko, can you hear me? What are you made of? I see you now—you're fearful underneath all the defenses and judgments. . . .

I've known you for a long time. At least I've known your judgments and defenses. But I don't know your fears. . . .

You're so quick to put up a defense—almost as quickly as if your hand were on a hot flame, but you don't think. Why do you feel attacked with no attacker?

Keiko-I fear the danger.

Beverly-What danger?

Keiko-The tearing down of my soul, of annihilation. . . . I am fearful of condemnation and judgment. That's why I judge.

Bev-What's the opposite of judging? It's mercy. How does mercy fit in? It's the release from judgment. You need mercy to rise above your judging and your fear of condemnation.

LET ME BE KEIKO (1996)
>   Keiko has mercy on my feelings,
>   Whether mean or nice.
>   She listens and accepts the truth.
>   With love, she faces vice.
>
>   Whether I am glad or sad,
>   She'll love me just the same.
>   Accepting self and others,
>   She never gives out blame.

If Keiko were a Teddy Bear she would be composed of mercy. Mercy for herself and others. When I hit rock bottom, Keiko's mercy finds me. No doubt, without her mercy, I could not rise above my shame.

"Lisa"
(Drivenness Versus Kindness)

I discovered Lisa, Tammy, Rebeccah, and Leah within 24 hours of each other. Each discovery was like an explosion in a mining dig that blasted out stubborn bedrock and lay bare delicate gems for the first time. The only trouble was that my mind felt nearly blown apart by each discovery. Yet the discoveries kept coming fast!

Old Lisa is a driven, anxious part of me. She feels unrest and guilt if she's not constantly running from one task to another. The pressures on her are endless. Satisfaction from a job well done is nonexistent.

In the following dialogue on May 5, 1996, I faced the Lisa part of me and named her.

DIARY ENTRY (5/5/96)

Bev-Who are you, Lisa? I see that you are driven. You are running from feeling bad and rejected. I know you well—you are my life! You are me! Instead of creating distance between us, I will sing you a song. . . . I will name you Lisa, because you're like Liz, who is now strong and smart, and you can be, too. You're not bad. You're not rejected. What would you like to be?

Lisa-Loved and secure.

It's funny how a simple thing can go a long way. One day the Old Lisa part of me felt painfully inadequate with no relief in sight. I stopped my high-pressured drive of running from task to task. Still I couldn't find peace. Then someone did one small and simple act of kindness for me and my pain dissolved, as explained in the following diary entry.

DIARY ENTRY (6/5/96)

Bev-Hi Lisa! We felt stupid and ridiculed, and we bounced back to feeling good by someone doing us a kindness. The same thing happens when we do a kind act for someone else. It doesn't matter which direction the kindness goes. It heals the embarrassment and the shame either way.

Lisa's sorrow, which she tends to run from, can be deep. One day, in a "driven" mode, I pushed myself on for hours while suffering from physical pain. Finally I gave up and collapsed on the couch, feeling guilty for stopping my work. Each time I tried to rise, a headache pounded me off my feet. I felt self-blame for getting a headache. I thought,

"I must have done something wrong." The following poem further describes the incident:

THE HEADACHE (2/29/96)
    I worked hard and got a headache—
    "You're such a bad, bad, soul,"
    Subconscious voices put me down
    Until there came a lull.

    Then Heavenward I pleaded-
    "Heal my hurting heart!
    Forgive me for overdoing,
    For not being very smart."

    Gently Heaven's answer came—
    "It's not as it may seem.
    You hurt not from overdoing,
    But from pain you did not glean."

"And I won't leave you comfortless.
I will help you find
The way to peace and healing
That will help your struggling mind."

DEGRADATION & KINDNESS (9/28/96)

A little bit of kindness
Is all that I need,
When degrading voices
I start to heed.

If I take one's kindness
Into my heart,
Like dew before sunshine,
Cruel voices depart.

There's kindness from friends,
That I can recall.
And I can be kind,
'Til there's no guilt at all.

DIARY ENTRY (1996)

Bev: Dear Lisa, I'm sick, so I'm not driven. Yet when my strength returns, because of you, I will be better at pacing myself and being easy going. You've taught me that one simple act or thought of kindness enables me to step out of a harried frame of mind and into a peaceful one.

From attempting to heal Lisa, I've learned to give more kindness to myself. But I easily forget. If Lisa were a Teddy Bear, she would be small enough to sit on my shoulder and whisper in my ear. She'd say, "Be kind! Be kind to the first creature you see! In thought, in deed, be kind."

"Tammy"
(Perfectionism Versus Reaching Your Own Goals)

Tammy was discovered in May of 1996. Tammy is an unsatisfied part of me who tries to please other people without really knowing what they want, and without being able to please them in a way that makes her feel better. Tammy has a hard time realizing that she can reach her fullest potential by pleasing her own heart.

> PERFECTIONISTIC TAMMY (2/26/99)
> Tammy feels driven
> To reach others' goals.
> However she prospers,
> No peace she knows.
>
> When someone has problems
> She thinks she's to blame.
> She'll only be happy
> Making her goals her aim.

I want to be a good mother, but when I blame myself for a child's misbehavior, I've side tracked from helping the child, to condemning myself as in the following illustrations.

> MY THREE-YEAR-OLD* UP FOR CRITIQUE (8/20/96)
> Silly, it hurts that Gi** withholds love
> From the sweetest toddler that I can think of.
>
> She calls him "Bad boy". 'Says he's impolite.
> She'd structure his manners and bedtime at night.
>
> Matt is afraid. He can't tell if she jests.
> When she puts him down, I felt quite depressed.

She says, "Greg's not strict, and neither are you.
Look at the things that you let Matt do.

You must have done something wrong in past days
For all of your teens should improve in their ways".

I hate me. I love me. I'm in a jam.
I hate the defensive girl that I am.

I love the woman, unruffled by words,
Kindness, respect, and strength she girds.

Oh that is who I wish I could be.
But my heart sunk as Gi spoke to me.

I won't lose hope, and shame self this time.
I'll love and respect this small son of mine.

I'll work out my feelings, all jumbled inside
That sap my strength as they silently hide.

These feelings, so awful, say I am bad, too.
But I can't judge me bad, or I won't get through.
*(my youngest child, Matt)
** (one of our foreign exchange students)

FEELING GUILTY (8/20/96)
Feeling guilt for all the trials
My family sees again,
Keeps me from the love I need
To let God's sweet hope in.

Hope for me and hope for them
And love and faith to try,
Are what we need, not blame and doubt,
Or else we can't get by.

WHOM SHOULD I PLEASE? (3/14/99)

When I seek to "please others"
It seems I am lost.
How can I be happy?
My soul pays the cost.

I'll only be 'me',
And do the most good,
If I seek the path
That I think 'I' should.

Nearly 30 years ago, I was aware of Tammy's characteristics of perfectionism and self blame. In the diaries I kept in my teenage years I wrote the following.

DIARY ENTRY (1964, age 11)

I've got to try harder to do everything better. I'm not good enough. If only I could study harder, (I was already an excellent student), and pray harder (I already prayed on my knees each morning and night), and spend more time helping my younger brothers and sister. (I was already spending time helping them daily.) I feel like I'm not good enough. I've got to try harder.

DIARY ENTRY (1968)

"I'm troubled by my self-righteousness. I want so much to stop it. . . ."

DIARY ENTRY (12/25/98)

In my young adult years, when I played with children, (and I was blessed with several), I was at ease. But when my thoughts turned to adult interactions, I grew troubled and frightened. Distance seemed to grow between myself and other adults because of expectations that I imagined they had for me. I try to not think they are in control of me, but sometimes I relapse. I need to seek what 'I' want, which gives me peace. I lose a part of myself by trying to be a 'stereotype'. I find myself by being 'me'. By reaching for 'my' goals.

TAMMY PERFECT (1997)
Tammy Perfect,
Here's a lie—
"Your achievements
Rank quite high!"
"I'm impressive.
Yes, that's I."
(You'd see sorrow
If you'd pry.)

TAMMY PERFECT (1996)
Tammy perfect,
Watch the kids.
Tammy perfect,
Canning lids.

Tammy perfect—
Pick the chard.
Tammy perfect—
Clean the yard.

Tammy perfect
Mustn't rest.
Tammy perfect
Fails the test!

She feels bad.
But she tries still
To find her worth
Through each new skill.

HOPE (1996)
I'm looking for hope,
A flickering flame.
If I try I am sure
I will find it again.

When I faced problems,
I believed I was bad.
Shame, unrest,
And pain I had.

I can't get better
When I blame me.
I just need love,
And sympathy.

SELF-BLAME VERSUS PEACE (1996)
God restored my peace of mind
When I lost two good rhymes.
Though nothing's left to show for them,
Inside, my heart's more kind.

I ask my God so often
To help my heart to see
When something's wrong and I feel bad,
I shouldn't be blaming me.

The flip side of "Perfection"
Is I'm always falling short.
I've only got to do my best.
Self-blame I must abort.

DIARY ENTRY (5/6/96)

Bev-Dear Tammy, I don't know the real you, just the part who worries and frets about things being perfect, with agony and fear. It seems to hurt you to think of things being less than perfect. Are you inferior?

Tammy-Yes.

Bev-Do you think the clean house will make you more worthwhile?

Tammy-Yes and no. Yes it can, in my pretending mind, but not in reality. 'Inferior' is my name.

Bev-Why do you feel inferior?

Tammy-I've learned it somewhere. But it doesn't make me happy.

Bev-Me neither. Let's say we oust that standard of perfectionism and replace it with something better.

Tammy-But with what? . . . I'm afraid. I'm afraid of being controlled and constrained.

Bev-But you have a choice—a choice to replace perfectionism with the hope of personal fulfillment.

DIARY ENTRY (5/19/96)

Bev-I feel too exhausted to do anything this morning, but the guilt for doing nothing churns me up inside.

Tammy-You agonize over your plans. You feel so inferior. That's the "perfect" side of me. Dump her.

Bev-Yes. I can see it now. My motivation for doing stuff while feeling ill, was out of inferiority and guilt, and feeling "bad". Tell me again how self-fulfillment works.

Tammy-Don't do what the other person says! Do what your heart believes is right.

Bev-Gotcha. Thanks.

I did not know nor plan that different parts of my personality would emerge. It just happened as a way of survival. And it's been a means of growth and comfort, and deliverance from old inhibitions. Were Tammy a bear, she would not have a push button to make her walk. She would not have a pull string to make her talk. She would be alive and free. A child would delight in her spontaneity and uniqueness.

"Rebeccah"
(Seeking Love Versus Giving Love)

I discovered Rebeccah on May 5, 1996. Rebeccah is needy for and searching for love. Sometimes Rebeccah (which means "ensnarer") desires love from unrewarding sources. This only adds to her empty feelings.

DIARY ENTRY (12/25/98)

One night two years ago, shortly after recognizing this needy part of me, I took a long walk with my husband. I remember sharing my feelings with him. It was a relief to get them out. I expressed the pain of wanting love in the wrong places and of my perpetual neediness. I then experienced a feeling of acceptance and compassion toward myself in the place of my former guilt. Perhaps I felt love for myself. It preceded a moment of revelation. From one step to the next a change came over me. I could see the answer to my neediness clearly: *Give love! Whenever I ache to receive love, give it!* The answer is so simple, yet so freeing from the bonds of neediness. Even if I'm hurting, I can love. Love first, and the pain dissipates second. It takes faith, but having practiced it for two years since that night, I've found that loneliness and sadness disappear when I forget myself and just give love to the other person. The way I change Rebeccah's neediness is simple, yet dramatic.

DIARY ENTRY (12/26/98)

I cherish the friendships I have, especially with my immediate family and my relatives. There seems to be a permanency to our belonging and our love. But yesterday, one of my relatives made me the brunt of jokes around the Christmas dinner table in front of family and friends. I had to struggle very hard to rise above a self-abasing relapse that their jokes brought on. I tried to pull myself out of self-centered thoughts by writing, and I wrote the following poem.

FEELING DESPISED (12/25/98)
   Being made fun of hurts,
   Unless love makes it safe.
   When jokes are made and laughs ring out
   It must be in good faith.

   Then my love just deepens.
   Fondness overrides.
   But when the jokes aren't told with love
   I think that I'm despised.

   Why think someone puts me down?
   What harm done if they do?
   God, my friend, sees in my heart.
   He knows if I am true.

   How do I internalize
   The scorn that's aimed at me?
   I'll not judge nor fret
   What their intent may be.

   Instead I'll pray for them,
   A contrite, humble plea.
   And if my prayers can't soften them,
   Perhaps they'll soften me.

DIARY ENTRY (12/26/98)

I felt kindly when today started, until new references were made as to how much I had been put down yesterday at our Christmas dinner table. Self-abasement soared, then self-control and mercy ruled. Back and forth like a yo-yo. Other happenings this morning showed me how accommodating I am when under fire. Accepting anger and standing up for myself don't come easy for me. Nor does it come easy for me to adopt an independent way of thinking, such as: "I couldn't care less what you think!" I have nothing to teach here. I have everything to learn.

ASHAMED/COMPASSIONATE (6/22/96)

I have one side that's needy.
It aches and yearns for love.
Always hungry, never full,
It's lies that it's made of.

I have one side that's giving.
Patient, full of love.
It fills me with such wonder.
Of heaven it's made of.

LOVE (5/6/96)

Rebeccah, Rebeccah,
Why do you hide?
You think you've got nothing
Of value inside.

You've lived by a lie—
That you'd be loved never.
But now it is time
That you and lies sever.

Rebeccah, I'm asking,
What do you need
To free you from lies
That hurt and deceive?

Rebeccah, Tell me of love,
All that you know.
Assure me that love's
More strong than its foe.

REBECCAH (6/9/96)
    A reaching to take,
    A reaching to give.
    A person who's dying,
    Or one that can live!

    When I reach to take,
    The pain runs so deep.
    Yet the joy in the giving
    Can make my heart leap.

If Rebeccah were a child's Teddy Bear, like the 'Velveteen Rabbit', it would be very flexible and very worn. It would also be very loved. I think the 'Velveteen Rabbit' said it well: "Love makes us real."

"Leah"
(Vanity Versus Being Yourself)

After discovering Leah on Monday, May 6, 1996, I was emotionally drained. I had discovered, named, and started talking to six parts of myself in just a few short days: Friday-Pacita; Saturday-Cara; Sunday-Keiko and Lisa; Monday-Tammy, Rebeccah, and Leah! I felt I couldn't take any more excitement and I begged God for relief. And relief did come. After Leah, I had a breather from discovering more multiple personalities for a while.

Leah has two aspects to her personality. First, she would feel inferior, rejected, and worthless. Second, she would build herself up in her mind so she seemed superior, and deserving of recognition.

> PAIN (10/26/96)
> I don't understand
> This subject very much.
> I can meet it two ways—
> Run, or feel its touch.
>
> I'm often running from it
> Not knowing it is there,
> Running to my house of shame,
> Or pride up in the air.
>
> But there's a hallowed moment,
> Painful, but so real.
> It's when I touch the pain,
> And then I start to heal.

REALITY (1996)
    I wouldn't face problems.
    I wouldn't face pain.
    I'd run until
    I went insane.

    To stop my pretense,
    To cease to flee,
    I face myself—
    Reality.

    For I'm not bad,
    In my heart I know.
    I needn't prove worth.
    I need no "show."

Conversations with Leah, and my other splits, led me to face my real emotions, as in the following dialogue.

DIARY ENTRY (5/6/96)

Bev-Leah, I hate you! Really, I feel sorry for you. . . . and for me.

Little b-Leah, you're struggling with an obsession about how you appear to people you barely know and to masses of people in your imagination who are watching you critically.

Bev-Leah, you can't be yourself when situations trigger this obsession.

Liz and Pacita-Leah, can't you replace these self-conscious thoughts?

Leah-I hate you all! I am pride! I do everything right. I am above you and want nothing to do with you.

Cara-Leah, you feel so low that you put up a front. It will hurt, but you and I can face the low feelings together. Can you imagine yourself stripped of pride, and as a precious being full of worth? Can you imagine that? Leah, I feel others are watching too, but they're not. It's all our imagination.

Leah-I can't imagine I'm of worth when I'm stripped of pride . . . except a little bit.

Keiko-Leah, I'm sorry I've added to your plight with my judgmentalness.

Leah-That's O.K. You're my friend. We worked together to build up a prideful image of me. But now you've changed. . . . And I will, too.

MORE ABOUT LEAH

The cover up of Leah's feelings is founded on lies. It's a lie that she is worthless unless she "excels". The focus of her efforts to earn a sense of worth by being better than others is a cruel trick. No matter how hard she tries, she'll never feel she's good enough.

The real Leah is concerned with being herself, not with what others think. She doesn't need outside validation.

At times of abasement, (by myself or others), it would be wonderful to feel a hug from an imaginary Teddy Bear Leah, who always loves me, just as I am!

"Jamie"
(Offensive Versus Forgiving)

DIARY ENTRY (5/10/96)

Jamie is like a rebelling adolescent. She is nicknamed "the protector" because she denies her painful feelings to protect another. As a result, pain fills her heart. She feels shame for having the pain. She labels herself bad for feeling pain. She's afraid to believe that someone close to her may be wrong. She's afraid to disagree and blames herself for others' faults. Jamie believes she must not have anger. She hates herself and wants to die when she does feel angry. Jamie is changing. She is starting to rebel.

DIARY ENTRY (5/10/96)

Beverly-When something happened that hurt, you didn't consider that the other person might be wrong.
    Jamie-No.
    Beverly-How did you perceive your hurt feelings?
    Jamie-I perceived sadness was from me not living right, so I tried harder to do what was right.
    Beverly-Your words make me feel very sad.
    Jamie-Why?
    Beverly-A part of you was imprisoned, a feeling part. If you can't feel and accept your feelings, you can't be totally real. Feeling sad makes you real.

DIARY ENTRY (5/6/96)

Bev-Please help me. Show me who you are.

Jamie-I am feelings denied to protect another.
Bev-Any kind of feelings?
Jamie-Feelings of my heart.
Bev-Fondness, despisement, favor, fear?
Jamie-Yes and more.

Bev-No wonder I first envisioned you as the fake—trying to behave so that others would like you.

Jamie-I did it because I'd been taught to please everybody-

Bev-And deny yourself. Why do you try to please people instead of honor your feelings?

Jamie-My feelings, I've been taught, are bad if they're not the way they're supposed to be—the way the other person decides my feelings should be.

Bev-You guess what the other person wants. You're not even sure of the other person's feelings. . . . Jamie, you don't have to do what others want! What would happen if you followed your own feelings?

Jamie-I need permission.

Bev-What if I gave you permission? Whatever you feel, it's not bad. It's not for denying. It's for passing through, or riding on, or treasuring forever. Jamie, you are your feelings. That's your substance deep inside—your feelings. And they're good. You needn't be ashamed.

Later-

Bev-Do you have any problems with the other person feeling differently than you?

Jamie-I have conflicting commands-honor my feelings and honor theirs.

Bev-Who told you to honor theirs?

Jamie-My superiors told me.

Bev-I'm sorry, but they were wrong. Do you believe in Jesus?

Jamie-Yes.

Bev-Try to please him. He's the only one you can trust. And he'll want you to honor your feelings as I do. Do you feel loved?

Jamie-I don't love myself. Other people love me.

Bev-Their love can come or go. Love yourself. Honor yourself. You must be your #1 self-respecter. No one else can respect you as much as you can. . . . Tell me about love.

Jamie-Whatever the other person wants, you give.

Bev-I hate learning painful stuff! My pain is all pressed together inside of me, and it hurts. Why do you think love is pleasing the other person? Who told you that?

Jamie-Satan.

Bev-Anyone else?

Jamie-I grew up with it being so.

Bev-How can I teach you of real love?

Jamie-Love me.

Bev-I'm happier now. Loving you will be fun!

DIARY ENTRY (11/17/98)

In reviewing this section of my book, I triumph. For months, thoughts of finishing this chapter filled me with fear. I couldn't even think of Jamie without fear. I recalled a broken window, roaming the streets barefoot in the night, crouching between parked cars in hiding with a suicide plan should anyone try to approach me. I recalled having a complete lack of trust toward every living soul. My memories have faded though. I have not been like that for several weeks.

DIARY ENTRY (1/15/99)

My most recent alter episode, ending a week ago, did not seem to be Jamie by name but I took on her way of thinking. It was life threatening and more unbearable than usual. I'm getting worn down by this alter business. My relapse was harder to endure. But I learned from it. I started voicing my thoughts to my husband. When I prayed about separating from him to protect myself from the stress and conflicts swirling in my mind, I received a change of heart. I resumed interaction with my husband and found I could not respectfully hear my husband out without expressing just how 'I' felt too. When I expressed my feelings sincerely, I found the ability to trust in my husband's sincerity.

...Recently the police thought my jogging husband was a murder suspect running away from the scene of a crime that Greg knew nothing about. They almost shot him as he jogged, because he's deaf in one ear and didn't hear their call to "Stop!" When they finally got his attention, he stopped and they treated him rough and held several guns to his head. When Greg told me about it, I was mad, but turned the anger on myself. I was afraid to be mad. I felt frustrated and helpless.

Here is one last poem about Jamie, trying to heal the wounded parts inside.

> JAMIE MY FRIEND (9/9/96)
> I've blamed myself for feeling sad.
> It was subconscious, too.
> I didn't know the way to glad,
> Nor what I ought to do.
>
> Now loving arms surround me.
> They reach into my soul.
> Accepting sad without the guilt,
> Jamie helps me so!

The two of us together
Can rise and face the day.
A comfort to each other,
When feelings turn so gray.

Unhealed Jamie can be a sleeping "bear" whose awakening is awful. Yet healed, Jamie forgives, loves, and accepts both others and herself. I'd like to picture Jamie as a bear giving itself a hug or if its seams rip and stuffing starts to come out I'd picture God's arms around it, holding it together.

"Emily"
(Loneliness Versus Reaching For Your Dreams)

Emily is a part of me who is afraid to reach for her hopes and dreams.

> HURTING FEELINGS (3/23/96)
> I'm too depressed to write,
> Too lost to search my heart.
> Exhaustion 'til I scream in pain
> Plays the biggest part.
>
> If I searched for reasons
> Why I lay here and cry,
> Could I ease my sadness?
> I'd really like to try.
>
> "Scrutiny" engulfs me-
> If I choose this way or that,
> I am guilty either way,
> My confidence laid flat.
>
> And if a thrill enfolds me,
> "Chastisement" eats it up,
> And "Shame" for feeling happy.
> Aloneness makes it tough.
>
> If I've strong desire,
> And longing deep within,
> There's "Judgment" for the hope I feel.
> Yes, "Shamefulness" again.

Whatever hurts me badly,
Whatever fears I feel,
Are not released for "Invalidate"
Tells me they're not real.

I'm overwhelmed with failure
To rise and be myself.
But I keep trying anyway,
Praying for God's help.

EMILY'S PRAYER (1998)
Lord, I write this poem with thee.
I find solace on bended knee.
My eyes dry, my heart dead,
No desire left to give:

I'm afraid someone will tell me
To stop crying, to stop feeling.
But in order to be real,
You seem to say: "Feel the pain."

Father, teach me how.
I fear. But I don't fear Thee.
Lead me to who I can trust—
Perhaps myself.

ALONE (5/10/96)
Emily is real.
Emily feels sad.
Coming from deep down
Something's hurting bad.

Emily don't care
If no one else is near.
Safer all alone,
No reprimand to hear.

DIARY ENTRY (6/5/96)

Beverly-Dear Emily, you are so young. What can I do to help you?

Emily-I am young, nearly infantile and I need permission for my feelings.

Beverly-How old are you?

Emily-About three.

Beverly-What can I do to help you take back your right to feel?

Emily-I don't really remember having it.

Beverly-You've practiced shame and denial for your feelings for so long. Have I started helping you to honor and accept your feelings?

Emily-In a wobbly way . . . And you need my help.

Beverly-How can you help me?

Emily-By helping you honor and accept yourself.

Beverly-This is hard. How do I do it?

Emily-It's not easy. You do it through each poem, each song, each offering of your love-filled heart to another, each prayer, each gift of solitude or of nature you enjoy, each forgiveness of another, each quiet, peaceful moment. Clothed in hope and patience, this is how you'll come to honor and accept yourself, and it takes a long time, I don't know how long.

Beverly-Enduring my worthless feelings longer will hurt.

Emily-Endure.

Later–

Beverly-Emily, writing to you keeps me from self-abasement. Jamie said she'd help my ache go away and then she turned me over to you. I feel frustrated. I keep setting my goals aside to sacrifice my heart for other people's petty desires. I need your help. I love your up front, honest, determined, relentless "three-year-old ways". If I had the determination of a three-year-old, nothing would stand in my way. I appreciate you.

Emily-I am so sad. I am not that strong, persistent child you see. I was once, but now I need you to make those qualities live in me again.

SOARING (1996)
>Last night I called my brother.*
>I'm glad for what he knew.
>We talked about an hour.
>From him much strength I drew:
>
>In youth he dreamed of taming birds.
>Scorned, he ignored the hurting words.
>He kept his dreams in spite of foes.
>Now he flies rare birds in shows.
>
>I see my way! I've figured it out!
>I'll reach for my dreams and my heart starts to shout!
>Whatever I want, whatever I feel,
>Makes me who I am! My dreams make me real!
>God, help me pick up those dreams in my heart,
>Brush off the cobwebs, and in my flight start.

* (My brother-in-law Martin Tyner, author of "Healer of Angels," and founder of "Southwest Wildlife Foundation")

SAD (12/2/96)
>Darn me—I'd like to be a dirt clod,
>All bunched up and small and cold.
>Where no one would touch or see me,
>Where I could die untold.

> But I'm warm and flesh, and feeling pain.
> I'm torn and ragged inside.
> God help me hold together.
> I can't find a place to hide.

I'M STILL REAL (1998)
> A sadness rises from my heart.
> I'm too fatigued to feel.
> I'm deadened by my medicine.
> But tears say, "I'm still real."

DIARY ENTRY (1/28/99)

Emily is a child filled with guilt for trying to be herself. Like Jamie, I fear Emily may not be healed. I wonder if my episodes with alters will go away on their own or if they will get worse, or if therapy will help. I'm opposed to therapy presently, with my psychiatrist, for talking about recent episodes gives me fear. Last time I spoke of an alter to my psychiatrist, all of a sudden I behaved destructively and threw something across the room. It seemed I changed into a different personality. I'm avoiding exploring alters with him to keep myself safe.

If healed Emily were a Teddy Bear, she'd excite me by reaching for the dreams in my heart.

"The Eagle"
(Acceptance and Comfort)

My favorite imaginary friend is a friend outside of me. He loves me, encourages me, and accepts me. He has unfaltering confidence in me. I call him the Eagle. I pretend the Eagle is who my husband will be in the eternities. When I feel very alone, misunderstood, and painfully unworthy, I think of the Eagle and I know I'm loved. At the same time, my trust and closeness to my husband is deepening. As I feel my husband's love and kindness and acceptance like never before, he seems to merge with the 'Eagle' in my mind. And Greg seems amused and entertained by my talk of this 'Eagle' whom he is becoming.

WARMTH AND LOVE (2/8/96)
>The Eagle forgives me
>And wraps me in care.
>He never condemns me.
>He just wants to share—
>
>His love and affection
>Forever with me.
>His strength lifts my soul,
>And heals soothingly.

ENLIVENED (2/10/97)
>Enlivened and happy
>I'm walking in joy,
>The Eagle right with me,
>My whole soul to buoy.

My every action
Is blessed and made light.
My heart feels more radiant.
My plans are more bright.

Excited and carefree,
And so much in love,
Transformed by your warmth,
You're what dreams are made of.

When my medicine wasn't working well, I felt abnormal guilt over everything and anything. Normal attraction to men made me struggle with feelings of badness. But the Eagle reassured me.

TO THE EAGLE (1997)
Hello Eagle, keeping watch over me,
Human, I'm being whatever I be.
Your love comes down, penetrating the skies.
I know between us there aren't any lies.

Shame for my day dreams dissolves with my tears.
Feeling your love melts away my fears.
You love me, accept me, and you understand.
I know around you, I'm loved just as I am.

REFUGE (6/24/98)
Eagle! You're my brightest hope!
My refuge from sore pain!
I longed for love where it is not,
An aching heart again.

I tried to look elsewhere for strength,
But I could grasp no balm
For hurt and ache and sorrow,
Until you came along.

You're perfect as a source of love,
Constant, kind, and true,
Spotless, forgiving, comforting,
And Greg's becoming you.

Sometimes I need more comfort
Than mortal souls can give.
My burden's lifted up by those
Who past earth's limits live.

The Eagle is intimate, compassionate, and encouraging. He completely understands me. He has bottomless faith in me. He overlooks my weaknesses. Yet he has none himself. To me, he is Greg, in the never ending hereafter. At times he and Greg seem to merge. I can't seem to picture the Eagle as a Teddy Bear. I imagine him to be free and awesome, like an eagle!

OUTLINE B
A SIMPLE CREED

Outline B is a simple creed to live by, based on what I've learned from coping with multiple personalities. One of my therapists was impressed with my creed. She said it would be good if the general public adopted it.

LITTLE B
Try to be sincere, to trust, and to love.

LIZ
Be firm, assertive, and uncompromising over your principles.

PACITA
Value your own opinion, as well as the other person's.

CARA
Accept your feelings compassionately.

KEIKO
Realize you and others will never be perfect. Have mercy for yourself, and others.

LISA
If you are feeling 'driven', stop to do a kind deed or to appreciate another's kindness.

TAMMY
Don't live a "perfectionistic" lifestyle according to someone else's standards. Do what you believe in!

REBECCAH
Don't seek love. Give love.

LEAH
Don't try to impress people. Just be yourself.

JAMIE
Negotiate with kindness. If another person is wrong extend kindness anyway, while still respecting your own principles.

EMILY
Reach for your dreams.

THE EAGLE
Look to a loving God for comfort and encouragement.

Some people may do these things naturally. But I believe I'm not the only one who doesn't.

CHAPTER 3

The Old Gray Mare Just Ain't What She Used To Be

A RACE HORSE
    Just as a race horse
    Meets days of glory,
    I'll share my success,
    As I tell my story.

    Along with success,
    Comes failure and pain.
    Good spells and bad spells
    Are part of the game.

    At length some horses
    Are turned out to pasture.
    Wiser, not prouder.
    Slower, not faster.

In this chapter I'll share some of my life's rises and falls. From childhood days when I tried to revive dead gophers, through college days when I outran the boys in my track class. To when I temporarily left my family during my mid-life struggles to detour personal suicide, to the present day when

I'm volunteering in Matt's first grade class days, and fighting imaginary foes in my karate class, nights.

MY ROOTS

My dad's father herded sheep in the mountains as a child. No other human around for miles. He told me he was afraid of cougars, and that he was unable to keep them from stealing lambs. Years later, he married a World War One nurse. They raised four boys while they both were teaching school. Their high-achieving eldest son Pat suffered a breakdown in his twenties. He was treated with strong drugs for schizophrenia and put in a mental hospital for over a year. It had to do with the breakup of his marriage, and how he tried to save his marriage and failed. Last month Pat shared with me memories of how horrible it felt to be drugged so bad that he was rendered entirely useless. Then a Dr. Owens diagnosed him as having manic depression (the former term for bipolar) instead of schizophrenia and gave him a new drug called lithium. Twenty-eight years later Uncle Pat still has the same doctor prescribing the same no longer new medicine. And Pat's very happy he's had no more disconcerting symptoms since.

My mother's family, less educated, was hard working. Her orphaned father Sam sailed from Ireland to America as a young man. In his childhood home, they had never celebrated a holiday nor let the children eat meals before all adults had finished. My mother used that as an explanation for why her dad didn't come out on Christmas morning, nor open his Christmas presents when she was a child. By the time I was born, though, Grandpa Sam was all fun! He'd pick me up with his strong carpenter hands and pretend I was a board which he was nailing to the ceiling. In delight, I laid straight as a board as he lifted me to the ceiling with one hand. I loved to see the houses his strong hands built. I worshipped him. Mom's mother Della was one of fourteen children raised on a farm. When Della was a child, her father Phillip left his wife and children in charge of the farm while he served as a missionary for his church. His church mission ended early with his leg full of buckshot and a cane to last him the rest of his life. He kept a souvenir jar of seven bullets which the doctors removed. The remaining bullets in his leg didn't get in the way of a seemingly prosperous life for Phillip and his family.

In San Diego, California, Mom and Dad met and married.

They raised six children in Southern California while Dad worked as a banker and Mom as a homemaker. This year marks their fiftieth wedding anniversary.

Feelings about my parents bring a lump to my throat when I recall family hikes with Dad and all the interests he shared with us. I loved our coast to coast camping trips, Dad's big homemade firework shows, and Dad teaching us how to body surf in the ocean. Dad's love for the out-of-doors has settled in my heart, as deeply as it has in his. Give me a tent in a forest over a house in a city any day! And like my dad, if I get behind the wheel, worries fade away into the scenery. Mom, the primary disciplinarian, had a big heart. She was gracious, unselfish, and giving.

MY YOUTH

The following poem tells about my childhood. (I wrote it during a 'bout with insomnia.)

INSOMNIA (10/4/96)
   Sleep eludes me. I feel quite bored.
   I'll play with old thoughts from long ago stored.

   My brother put spiders in cups I drank from.
   My mom sewed all night 'til my prom dress was done.
   I've played with dead gophers. I've tried to gain weight.
   'Got stuck on a rooftop. 'Lied to teacher when late.

   I was hit by a car, being thrown through the air.
   'Sued for car damages. It didn't seem fair.
   Sweet 16 and never been kissed.
   'Would have stepped on the rattler if it hadn't hissed.

   I teepeed houses and didn't get caught.
   3.8 GPA, but forgot what was taught.
   I talked on the phone for an hour each day.
   For an hour each night my guitar I would play.

   I cried the most tears from a break up with Bob.
   Greg's jokes were so good I'd laugh 'til I'd sob.
   My first kiss from Greg, after Disneyland date.
   That ol' turtle joke* determined our fate.

   'One lung collapsed and the other near gone.
   'Engaged on a mountain top after hiking so long.
   I've sung in a prison. I've bathed in the mud.
   A kid broke the window when I was the sub.

   I refereed football, not knowing the rules.
   It got me a job in one of the schools.
   I almost got fired from slapping a face.
   The rude child had braces and I was disgraced.

I back up my car into fences and things,
For 25 years giving cars lots of 'dings.'
Bit by a dog and Eli's rabbit, too.
So sorry, Eli, we had rabbit stew.

Now comes the day with all of its light.
I'm gonna be tired. Up since midnight.

- (The Turtle Joke I told Greg before our first kiss: I introduced "Right Turtle" and "Left Turtle", pretending my hands were the turtles. I placed my 'turtle' hands on Greg's outstretched hands, side by side. An earthquake comes, forming a big crevice between Greg's hands, separating the two turtles from each other. The turtle's phone lines were knocked down by the earthquake, and the turtles had no way to contact each other. That was, until they found a way after a desperate search. My two turtle hands walked up Greg's two arms separately until they met behind Greg's neck and clasped together tightly. Then I asked "Are you sure you want to talk about turtles?" After that line, Greg clasped his hands around my waist and well, we didn't end up talking about turtles.)

FROM MARRIAGE TO SEVEN CHILDREN

The place was Sacramento, California. The year was 1977. I had just finished my second year of teaching at Merryhill Elementary School. My husband Greg was a graduate student at UC Davis. I was seven months pregnant. My husband picked me up from my last day of school teaching for an eight-hour drive to Los Angeles, for a long awaited vacation. In a few days I was alone in Los Angeles with a stomach ache while loved ones spent the day at Disneyland. I spent the day calling the Los Angeles Kaiser Hospital, confused as to whether or not I was in labor. Frustration over phone calls put on long holds did not match my frustration over being told that only my own doctor, back in the Sacramento Kaiser, four hundred miles away, could help me. He was unreachable by phone. That evening, my mom—who thought it was false labor—teased me for cutting short our visit, when Greg and I left Los Angeles and drove all night to the Sacramento Kaiser Hospital. There I delivered not the baby girl mother predicted", but "Timothy" and "Samuel" too. Premature, our twin babies' lives were in the balance for several weeks. I had taken fertility pills in order to get pregnant. I thought I felt eight limbs stretching inside of me. But my doctor did not think that I had 'two' babies instead of one—until they were on their way out prematurely. That was only the beginning to the series of unexpected things that parenthood brings. The following two years were happy years. In 1979 another son Eli was born which made our play with the twins even more fun. My happiness bottomed out with fatigue when I became pregnant with our fourth child, in 1980. Shaming myself for being so tired, instead of asking if I should try to not take on so much, was typical of my youthful sky-high perfectionism. I suppressed my feelings about my need for rest instead of asserting them. Then, exhaustion claimed me, and three years of happy play came to an end. Carefree excursions with a stroller full of children gave way to our stroller collecting dust. Our huge family garden, the train station with all its curiosities, the noisy duck pond, the winding creek with an abandoned canoe which Timothy always crawled into with glee, the market where we knew everybody, the campus hog farm, the nuclear lab where Greg showed us pictures of his experiments with protons shooting lithium and scattering neutrons—all these things went on without us. My happy stay in the world became confused. I didn't fit in like before. While others continued to function, I retired to bed and the children to babysitters. If I attempted a trip to the playground with the children, first, I faced the task of walking there which seemed insurmountable. Second, I faced the impossible task of holding my head up once we got there. My confusion continued as Greg worked long hours finishing his PHD in physics at UC Davis. Our fourth child, a most beautiful daughter Christy was born just before Greg graduated and selected a job offer near my hometown of Simi Valley, California. Then we enjoyed a company paid move over those same four hundred miles we had traveled while I was in labor with the twins. But this time we had a stop over at a fancy beachfront hotel, and the most relaxation I'd seen, or would see, for months. Greg loved his new job. And coming home to our four little ones every evening was all play for him. Yet, after our move, I sat and stared at the wall in a stupor of sadness frequently. I harbored animosity and ill will. A year later Greg admitted that during those days I had seemed like a witch and he felt like he would be miserable for the rest of his life. I saw my pastor once during this time, and when I mentioned my depression, he suggested a good therapist. For the first time in my life I saw a therapist, Larry Mansell, who probably would have been the best therapist of my life if I would have let him be. In 1980 I had two therapy sessions with Larry. During the first session I spoke hesitantly of my depression. During the second session I told him I was all better and bid him farewell. He said he was concerned about things he'd observed, beginning in my youth, he having been in my neighborhood for a long time. But I more firmly insisted that there was nothing wrong and said goodbye. I didn't trust therapists. First, my mom had taught me that therapists corrupt people. Second, I thought that to need his help would make me less of a person and I clung to a hope that there was nothing wrong with me. Years later, I wish I could talk to him, but he's long since moved away.

Actually, I did regain my physical health during the same period of time that I saw Larry Mansell and my marriage improved. "Fun" once more became a way of life. Homemade play dough with some food colorings topped any kitchen creation I could make. I didn't care that homemade bread dough got kneaded by eight little hands along with mine. I loved kids. My idea of a perfect day was a few sack lunches, well-conditioned preschool hikers, a stroller for the baby, and miles of sights on the way to the library, or to our favorite farmyard. Our days were topped off with watching for Daddy to turn off the freeway, and load us up into his station wagon on his way home from work. In 1982, when our twins turned five years old, we welcomed another daughter into our family, Butterfly. She was named Butterfly—by her two year old sister—after a butterfly-shaped cake given to us by a neighbor to celebrate her birth. A few weeks later, with an infant carrier against my chest, two toddlers inside the stroller, and the twins pushing our stroller, our daily excursions started early. We walked to Timothy and Samuel's kindergarten class every day. Although life grew complicated as the regimen and pressures of school made life more stressful, I still have their first sentimental kindergarten art creations hanging on my wall. In 1984 when the twins started second grade, I gave birth to my sixth child Phillip. Although I never regained a trim waistline again after Phil was born, our home has been filled with humor and laughter because of Phil. For fourteen years I have been enjoying his sense of humor. Phillip and I grew up through the years quite close, him being my last baby until 1992 when we had our seventh and last child, my angel Matt.

A BREAKDOWN (1986)

The year was 1986. The month was October. I'd gotten up by 6:00 AM to spend half an hour reading the scriptures and praying before the children got up. At 6:30 AM I was doing my daily 30 minutes of aerobics to a tape with my six children, ages two to nine, dancing with me. A pain in my soul pressed heavily on my mind. I shrugged it off as usual, or tried to. But by the day's end I had erupted like a volcano. After an all out wrestle with one of my sons, I seemed to have deeply plunged into insanity, confusion, and explosiveness. I locked myself in the bathroom for hours, tearfully praying for help.

The next day was a holiday and we had a picnic planned.

I painstakingly attempted to spread butter on the sandwiches but it seemed unbearably hard. I fell on the floor in a heap of exhaustion instead. Following were several nights of insomnia. I lost my ability to fully care for my children. After sleeping only 30 minutes one night, I was awakened by a dream replaying a moment of childhood molestation. I laid awake trembling, sweating, and then, at dawn, I called Dr. Chevy, my family doctor.

Dr. Chevy began seeing me regularly from that day on. I was diagnosed with clinical depression. For five years Dr. Chevy tried various medicines which I was non-responsive to. What helped me most was getting counseling—and taking a look at my feelings with compassion and hope. It would take a long time to overcome a deep sense of guilt I'd harbored since childhood.

MY ANGEL MATTHEW

After five years of depression I seemed to have completely recovered. I was thirty-eight, still on medication, and adding a four bedroom addition to our three bedroom home. I became pregnant with our last child, our angel Matthew. We also had two Indonesian foreign exchange students living with us at the time of Matthew's birth. Our family totaled eleven as I held my newborn infant in my arms at the hospital. OB Dr. Hope insisted I was rested enough to go home the day of the birth, until he observed a hospital visit from my children. With three young siblings climbing on my bed to fight over who gets to hold the baby, and a few siblings taking an interest in raising, lowering, bending, and straightening my bed, Dr. Hope decided to let me stay in the hospital an extra day, to give me a rest from what waited at home. In the following months, home front was bitter-sweet. The pains of family problems with the older teenaged children were softened by the love Matthew brought into our home. I lost much of my physical strength after Matthew's birth. I still tried to cook dinner every night, but I fell apart daily from the effort. I would not be defeated and change our tradition of eating dinner together, but my explosions and depression each night finally made me reconsider. I remember praying, "God, how do I get dinner on the table each night without losing my temper and storming out?" I felt in my heart His answer: "Don't cook. Don't even grocery shop." The woman's traditional role in the kitchen was so ingrained in me that nothing short of God himself could have made me voluntarily surrender it. Samuel wanted a job, so I hired him as cook—to pay for his hobbies of toying with engines and raising tropical fish.

The relief from cooking gave me a rest. I had new experiences—earthquake recovery from the '94 Northridge earth quake; giving in to some of my children's requests for home school; flying Cessnas piloted by my 15-year-old son Tim; and participating with him in a wilderness rehabilitation program for substance abuse. At times I bottomed out in exhaustion, though, and felt hopeless.

To make a long story short, I've had thirteen years, of depression—except for the year Matt (now 6 years old) was born. His presence has helped me stay alive. For recently, suicide has been an unrelenting temptation, but my love of Matt keeps pulling me through.

THE CROWN OF MY LIFE
    The crown of my life,
    Seems to be Matt.
    He's given me hope.
    I'm grateful for that.

DIARY ENTRY (Winter 1998)

This week, my first kindergartner Tim who is now six-foot-two dropped by and saw his 6-year-old baby brother reading a familiar book. "Hey! Matt's reading my first grade book!" And I realize through all the ups and downs, I'm glad to be going through it all over again. Though I am slowed down physically, my love for my kids is more. Before, I regularly tossed six kids in and about the grocery cart as naturally as tossing in groceries. (Yes, the kids got buried by groceries, but they were too young to care.) Now, Matt has memories mostly of Daddy grocery shopping with him, and of Mom waiting at home in bed, to read him stories.

The following poetry portrays these last few years of my life while struggling with depression.

GOOD SPELLS & BAD SPELLS
(written in 1999 about my horse, Jonny)
    An impressive thoroughbred
    Served me very well.
    Then he started spooking,
    And on my child he fell.

    I love my horse though he's unsafe.
    He seems somewhat like me.
    His unpredicted bad spells
    Negate his past glory.

YO-YO (1997)
    Retiring full of happiness,
    And love, and wondering why.
    Was this the end of my bad spell?
    I hoped new strength was nigh!

    Come morning, every sight and sound
    Were gifts to please my heart.
    Then quickly I fell to vexing pain.
    Ambitions now must part.

TIRED (1997)
    It's hard because I feel as if
    A complete rest would help,
    But I seem to wait on others
    Instead of on myself.

BURN OUT (1997)
    A beautiful home
    Is going to pot.
    Outings and errands
    Have cost me a lot.

I swam out too far.
I've gone in too deep.
I want to keep going,
But now I'm too weak.

WORDS UNSAID (1997)

I am not listening.
I'm blocking you out.
My frustration tolerance
Has all run out.

Not that you're erring,
Not that you're wrong.
I just don't know
Where my patience has gone.

Please don't touch me
While we talk.
I'll jump out of my skin,
My nerves are so taut.

No one's fault.
No one's cause.
My nerves are frayed.
Hot wires dance raw.

CONFLICTS OF TIME
(written about the time that I discovered
I was pregnant with Matthew)

We were building our addition,
Buying sinks and lights,
Painting and wallpapering,
Many pretty sights.

Then my strength stopped dead.
And I could do no more.
Another wee addition
To our family was in store.

I recalled a Promise,
From many years before,
Wrapped in inspiration
Of what might be in store—

It said if I got pregnant,
I could raise the other six.
But there was no guarantee
That this house I could fix.

'Twas hard to stop my painting,
But I sacrificed instead.
I just cared for the children,
Most the time from bed.

I've found that more than gourmet meals
The children need our time,
And listening, and heart-felt warmth,
And caring that they're fine.

Yet sometimes I would feel so ill
And cross while on my feet,
That my kids preferred me back in bed,
Listening, smiling, sweet.

DIARY ENTRY (1995)

We took a relaxing vacation with our four youngest children, leaving the oldest three at home alone. When our car pulled up in front of our house, I couldn't bear to walk in the front door and face the burdens of homemaking. It was a Sunday, so Greg was off work and free to take care of the kids, so without looking toward the house I just turned the other way and took a ten hour walk through the city. I walked for miles until I felt I could handle coming home. With seven kids, mostly teenagers, there would be stress, and my depressed mind did not feel very strong for handling stress.

REVERIE (1995)

I want to be alone
In my warm, soft room.
Don't make me talk to people.
I'll crawl into a womb.

Let me hear the dogs bark,
The squeak of Matthew's swing,
The leaves blown by the breezes,
The peace that nature brings.

RETREAT (2/99)

Away from home I get the gas,
Change the oil and tires at last.
This car's done. Go get the next.
Take Matt along. Much work. No rest.

Love for Matt brought out the sun!
We romped and played 'til day was done.
Then sleep claimed Matt, as home drew nigh.
Within a mile, I start to cry.

It hurts so much to go back home.
It's to my room to be alone.
Joy when gone! Pain when here.
Carefree steps, verses caution, fear.

I'D LIKE TO HIBERNATE (1998)
With Matt I'd like to hibernate,
In a cave for a reprieve.
I'd like the comfort of
A cocoon in which to cleave.

I'd go into a coma,
'Til strength is mine to keep.
I really would enjoy
A taste of some relief.

I pray for help refraining
From taking my own life.
Though tired and insane, I can't give up my fight.

DIARY ENTRY (10/7/98)

I'm presently sitting at the computer, my heavy head nestled in a pillow against the wall. I'm doubled over with cramping fatigue. Butterfly's boyfriend just totaled his truck an hour ago. Phillip's at the Doctor's with an infected boil, fetching a ride from our neighbor since Butterfly took my car. While I type, I'm giving six-year-old Matthew help with his homework. My husband's coming home late tonight, so I'll have to miss our new karate class. Yet, today is the first day in several in which I don't need to isolate myself in order to prevent violent or suicidal impulses.

THINGS THAT MAKE ME GLAD (1997)

I've kept intact my sanity.
I've kept intact my life.
Finally, I've found relief
From weeks of toil and strife.

It may be just a mood swing
That brings relief to me.
Still I want to count those times
That made me glad and free.

The first time, it was a song—
Country western and quite new.
It said to "Hold your head up
When the rain pours down on you."

The next time, 'twas a friendship
I struck up with a teen.
We were in the DMV,
Waiting to be seen.

We hit it off so warmly,
His youth, vibrant and bright.
Our talk was energizing.
All my cares grew light.

The third time made my glad heart swell—
I watched Christy's ballet!
In reverent awe I watched my daughter
Dance my cares away.

The following wraps up my life's story with illustrations about how I have adapted personally to the difficulties I face.

DIARY ENTRY (1998)

My husband asked me recently what I'd do with my life if I got well. I was surprised at how simple my heart's desires were! First, I said, I would cook! Then I would clean! Then I would plant a large vegetable garden. It's funny, my present hobbies of writing this book and dreaming of numerous others to write did not seem important to me anymore. Nor did all my song writing nor my musical pursuits to sing with a band or to pull off a musical CD with some friends. Taking my present drum and guitar lessons no longer seemed important. Nor karate. I just wanted to be a plain ordinary good mom and wife. Perhaps my creative pursuits were just a part of my sickness.

My heart's desire (above sickness or health, life or death) is to live true to Him I love the most—God. I don't have to be healthy to please Him. I only need to have a pure heart. And I'm learning to have a pure heart, not in spite of my depressive disorder, but because of it. Compassion, love, and mercy are developed not as a result of mental illness, but as the means to rise above it.

NEW THINGS IN STORE (1997)

Maybe I will never
Be cooking every night.
Maybe Matt will need day care
'Til he's a grown child's height.

Maybe exercise will be
A thing of touch and go.
Maybe chores and outings
Will see an all time low.

No more friends for barbecues,
With whom to take a swim.
Maybe I can't tidy house
The first time I begin.

Maybe planting strawberries,
And baking bread and more,
Are in my past, not future,
And new things are in store.

Supporting Greg in what he does
As he assumes my roles,
I give our kids a chance to see
How Dad keeps family goals.

Being restful, being quiet,
With Greg taking the lead.
Accepting all his efforts,
Goodwill is what I need.

The family but seems better.
Home hasn't lost its fun.
It's different with Mom's sickness,
But with love, home still can run.

Now I have different hobbies:
I'm always making jokes,
I teach Matt while lying down,
I welcome teenage folks.

With lighter work I have more time
New interests to explore.
There's love and learning in my heart.
I have new things in store.

RELAXING CONTENTEDLY (1996)
> Content to rest
> With slowed down stride.
> Full of warmth
> And love inside.
>
> Ashamed since I'm
> Too tired to work?
> No, I'll rest,
> And guilt I'll shirk.

HEAD DOWN (1996)
> Boy, do I feel glad!
> What a great mom my kids have!
> As long as I keep
> My head down when I speak
> I'm loving instead of a crab!*

* (For years, Butterfly said she preferred me lying down to standing, for then I was a better listener.)

TO THE SANDMAN (1:00 AM)
> Take me away!
> I've laid here too long,
> Curled up near Greg's warmth.
> Still mania's strong!
>
> Our night light is burned out.
> In darkness I write,
> In hopes you will claim me
> From mania's flight.

Oh Sandman, oh Sandman,
Put sleep in my eye.
I know I'm a hard case.
My mind's on a high.

My mind is a pasture.
Wild colts don't grow up.
I build better fences,
But they learn to jump.

I give up my efforts.
The keyboard is near.
The strains of a new song
My soul longs to hear.

There's juice in the kitchen,
And laundry to do,
Computer files waiting,
Some wood staining, too.

Each bait I will reel in
As minutes sail by.
Catch me on your next round.
Dear Sandman, goodbye!

THE OLD GRAY MARE
JUST AIN'T WHAT SHE USED TO BE (8/98)

Canning fruits and vegetables used to be a celebrated family activity in the late 70's. When my husband and I canned four hundred pounds of pears and peaches one summer, our family devoured them before the next season. In the 80's every Friday

I energetically scrubbed the house and the windows. In the early 90's we used to have barbecues weekly with our kids and their friends. But now the backyard barbeque is full of dust and spiders. Those days are over. Now our home has become a stopping point for teen friends who don't mind if I'm still in my pajamas at 2 p.m. We've had lots of teen parties where all I have to do is sit around and be a friend, for the teens prefer to do all the physical jobs themselves, right down to ordering the pizza and filling up the water balloons. We still host foreign exchange students, something we started in 1991. We've had students from as far north as Russia and Finland and as far south as Indonesia and Tasmania. When I was pregnant with Matt our Indonesian students Vivi and Tita experienced having our seven-year-old Phillip teach them how to microwave everything from oatmeal to hot dogs. They experienced going to the hospital to welcome our new baby who surprised us early. This year is my season to help in Matt's school—if it's the only thing I get out of bed for. Usually I communicate with Matt and listen to him read while I'm lying down. These days we live with a messier house and yard, children getting transportation from each other, and occasional periods when I am not accessible mentally. Yet more laughter, openness, and trust replace some of the stiff nervousness and fears of my younger years. Until my strength and sanity stabilize, I'm trying to be content with doing less. I try to be grateful for accomplishing just one thing each day.

CHAPTER 4

A Shrink In The Rink

For a decade, I've lived a few doors down from Tanya, a professional ice skater. Her coaches, and my therapists, have taught us techniques for many years. We learn. We try. We fall. We rise. We soar. Whatever setbacks we face, we never give up. When we must perform beyond our ability, we look to our coach for help.

A PUSH IN THE RIGHT DIRECTION (1981)

The first time that I became so depressed that I seemed to turn into a different person, was after my third pregnancy. I didn't have the strength to take care of my newborn, my one-year-old, and my three-year-old twins. My husband was wrapping up his doctorate in physics by working nearly sixteen hours a day. When he graduated from UC Davis, we moved to Simi Valley, California where he began working for Rocketdyne. It took me five months to find our silverware in moving boxes stacked in our living room. I watched our four preschoolers and nursed my baby without playing outdoors like I used to. I spent many hours with our children sitting on the couch with stories and songs; I fixed simple dinners of eggs, sandwiches, and pancakes; and I began to spend many hours just staring at the wall. For the first time in my life, I hit a child. I secreted my impulses to break windows. And much of my love for my husband died.

Then, I saw my bishop, Don Moberly. I was full of guilt for not being able to hold up better. Don consoled me. He commended me for what I was doing well.

He recommended I see a psychologist Larry Mansell for depression. Don's compassion and empathy toward me won my trust. Because I trusted him, I ventured out to see a psychologist for the first time.

TESTING THE ICE (1981)

I look back at my first professional counselor—Larry Mansell, as a very wise and insightful man. But after two visits, and significant improvement, I curtailed our visits against his advice. I was afraid of my family's disapproval of me getting counseling—especially my mother's. I wanted to pretend I was fine, and made myself believe I was fine. At the same time, I weaned my fourth baby, and started to gain control of my life again. (For pregnancies took a lot out of me, and nursing my babies exhausted me even more heavily.) However, I did take Larry's advice to take a vacation with Greg, without our children. Larry's daughter baby-sat our four preschool age children while we were gone. I was pleased with the improvement in my life.

Larry Mansell recommended I read "Eliminate Your SDB'S (Self Defeating Behaviors)" by Jonathan M. Chamberlain. Over the years I reread this book and it's techniques to help me: first, to overcome depression (1982); and then, in 1987, to overcome in a phenomenal way my habitual guilt over sex.

LONG-TERM SUPPORT (1985-1999)

In 1986—after a season of infertility—I couldn't hide my guilty feelings in motherhood anymore. Experiencing another stretch of infertility brought to the surface a destructive belief that

I was bad—even my self-loathing which had been formed during childhood trauma—which was crying out to be healed. Overnight, I switched from trying to hold everything together, to surrendering to my need for help. My husband took me to see our family practitioner, Dr. Chevy. When I left Dr. Chevy's office I had an antidepressant prescription and some literature about clinical depression. Dr. Chevy didn't see me recover from depression until briefly in 1991. He told me that he would ease me off of all my medicine in January of 1992. But I stopped my medicine on my own in December of 1991 when I realized that I was pregnant. 1991 was the last time I knew good health. I had my last baby, Matt, and with a houseful of teenagers, enjoyed him immensely! But I couldn't keep up with life. In exhaustion, I fell to depression again. And in 1993, Dr. Chevy referred me to a psychiatrist.

Dr. Chevy has continued to lend moral support. He cares, he has faith in me, and he has compassion. I wrote this poem about him after seeing him in his doctor's office for an appointment once:

DR. CHEVY (10/2/97)
>He treated me with kindness.
>I feel so warm inside.
>He loves and cares about me.
>His thoughts he didn't hide.
>
>He talked of my accomplishments
>As if he had all time.
>He told me: "Don't berate yourself."
>Encouragement I find.
>
>I shared with Dr. Chevy,
>My interests, and my joys.
>I felt his pat upon my back,
>His care was like a buoy.

THE WRONG COACH (1987)

In 1986, after three weeks of sleeping but a few hours a night, I faced my depression. One night I had slept only half an hour when a flash back dream of molestation woke me up, I told Doctor Chevy about the nightmare. He insisted I needed therapy. I was too mistrustful to try the Jewish psychologist—that Dr. Chevy highly recommended. I tried instead, an out of town Christian therapist from my own church. The therapist's name was Dr. Jones. He referred me to a book, "Getting to Know the Real You", by Sterling G. & Richard G. Ellsworth. Later, the book helped change my life. But Dr. Jones did not relate to me. He continually spoke of my need to forgive when I didn't even feel animosity. While I was hurting in my heart, he spoke of embarrassing scenarios which had nothing to do with me and which in no way helped me feel better. I stopped seeing Dr. Jones after a few sessions.

A TRUSTED COACH (1987, 1996)

After the Christian psychologist Dr. Jones lost my trust, I prayerfully mustered up the courage to see the Jewish psychologist that Dr. Chevy recommended. His name was Gary Golden. Since childhood—although I picked up many of my mother's good qualities—I had also picked up on her fears—which I turned into a mistrust of people who were different than me. But I'd become humbled enough to be open. I was ready to put my faith into Dr. Chevy's recommendation.

DIARY ENTRY (1988)

When my eyes first saw Gary Golden I was taken back by his aura of warmth, kindness, and compassion. Before our first words were spoken I felt comfortable and important around him. I saw Gary every week for a year. With his help I looked at how I denied my feelings. I began to accept my feelings and to accept and value my thoughts. After a year, Gary said that I still had a lot of emotional problems left to address. I stopped seeing him though, because after a year I began to feel a growing attraction to him and I couldn't deal with having feelings for another man besides my husband. I had been able to remain 'removed' from other people's hearts before my 1986 breakdown. But after the breakdown, I wore my feelings on my sleeve, and I often felt attraction for other men (until I later healed my split personality parts). I had never had that problem before my breakdown. It seemed a wall of holding back painful emotions had come down. I was no longer a 'Patti Perfect' fake. I was a real feeling person, vulnerable, confused, and struggling to deal with feelings I didn't know how to handle very well.

The year following my termination of visits with Gary was the blackest year of my life. The unyielding depression and daily thoughts of suicide only let up with time. The next four years I turned to books for help.

The following poem is one I wrote the year after I stopped seeing Gary. It was a year full of loneliness and despair.

> PUSH ALONG (1988)
>   Hard to write emotions,
>   Dammed up very high.
>   Guilt and pain and big goals
>   Are jumbled, so I sigh:
>
>   "I can't venture forward,
>   Until I see the way.
>   Perhaps it's just to push along
>   Through darkness every day."

Eight years later, when I was in a psychiatric hospital, I bumped into Gary Golden there, quite by accident. I hadn't seen him for several years. He asked why I was in Charter Hospital. I told him my car ran out of gas. He laughed, and we sat down and talked in the hospital dining room. His warmth and caring and laughter made our bumping into each other a happy moment during my stay in the psychiatric hospital. After my release, I saw Gary for several counseling sessions. Gary inspired me, mostly with his love, his good heart, and his compassion. To this day I keep in touch with Gary, and I regard him as a brother. I will always consider him a special friend.

DIARY ENTRY (10/5/98)

I just got off the phone talking to my friend Charity. She had fallen apart emotionally, under the pressures of lonely, draining days at home with several small children including twins. We understood each other over how difficult it is to be unable to cope with life. We both began therapy, ten years apart from each other, with two different Jewish psychologists. Charity too was leery at first of seeking help from a non-Christian therapist, her being a Christian like me. But we both agreed on the phone today that the therapy received from these two Jewish psychologists was life-saving. We had let painful emotions pile up until we exploded, and then collapsed. Our therapists helped us as we poured out our painful feelings that had been kept inside for so long. Charity and I had been raised in an era where problems were not talked about, but pushed under the carpet. Therapy was not easy for either of us. We had formerly learned how to ignore problems, not accept them. When we finally sought help, we were so severely depressed that I doubt we could have survived emotionally without the therapy. Talking with Charity was very comforting. We were open with one another. No need to censor our feelings with shame or fear.

SISTERLY HELP (1992, 1996-2000)

My two sisters have helped me. They've had struggles of their own. Recently we've set aside our emotional shields and grown more open and trusting with each other. One of my psychologists, Cheri McDonald is not a member of my family. Yet she seems like a sister to me. She's a solid member of my church, which lends to understanding when I divulge both rebellion and allegiance toward my religious upbringing. She's come to my home to meet with my family. She's helped me on the phone many times to work out about-to-explode emotions.

Cheri encourages me. When I share fledgling ideas, she applauds. She says I have excellent coping skills. She makes me feel intelligent and capable. She always applauds my decisions to protect myself from suicide or from being violent.

DIARY ENTRY (12/12/98)

Anger not allowed unless it's against myself can be a nightmare. I called my psychologist Cheri today, while she was out of state on vacation, because I needed her help. On the phone, she praised me for keeping myself alive and gave no quick answers to prevent self-destructive thoughts, but rather encouraged me to flee from the enactment of such thoughts now, and in the future. She encouraged me by saying that it would get easier with time.

DIARY ENTRY (11/17/98)

Cheri supported my decision to stop focusing on my misery by trying to think about someone other than myself. In the middle of my problems, I can enjoy a diversion of happiness, by being kind.

CHERI, PLEASE HELP ME! (5/5/97)

I like you because
You help me with Greg.
You help me when I
Have self-blame in my head.

It's so hard sometimes
To differ from Greg,
Without blaming me.
So I'll think instead—

Of past success,
Standing up for me.
Not bitter or blaming,
Just loving patiently.

JUMPS AND BUMPS (1994-1999)

Dr. Williams is the psychiatrist I choose in 1994 when Dr. Chevy recommended I find a psychiatrist for the first time. I chose Dr. Williams because his receptionist was kind. I had made inquiries about other psychiatrists but disliked the tone of their voices on their message machines. I also disliked getting call backs over a week later. Dr. Williams called me back within a day.

Dr. Williams treated me for depression at first, then for bipolar disorder. He prescribed lithium in 1995. Then he followed my case by regular phone calls when I uncomplyingly stopped all treatment and visits for a few months. The next time we met, I had lost strength to walk or eat. Greg carried me in his arms to my doctor who admitted me to Charter Psychiatric Hospital. I didn't learn much from being in the hospital except that I didn't want to go back. I concluded I must not quit taking Lithium or other meds without the supervision of my doctor—or I may end up completely drained of strength and hope. Yet Dr. Williams found me unusually unresponsive to medicine. We worked together to improve my medication and all but once I've taken exactly what he prescribed. Dr. Williams first tried the more standard medicines on me, followed by more specialized medicines. I have no more desire to write about my countless medications than I have desire to take them. I'm very tired of most of my medicines. By the time I finish this book my medicines will most likely be different. There's only one medicine I appreciate very deeply. It's curbed suicidal thoughts, auditory hallucinations, and feelings of despair. The medicine is "Risperdal".

MY HEAD (7/27/98)

> I have to take a Risperdal,
> And go to sleep right now.
> My head has too high voltage!
> I've lost my mind somehow.
>
> I want to scream! I feel my head
> Get fried from inside out!
> But all I really want to do
> Is calmly get about.

LIGHTNING AND THUNDER AND BROKEN GLASS (1998)

> Lightning and thunder and broken glass!
> I have got to find relief fast!
> I took 1/2 a sleep pill and went to bed.

And now mammoth screams explode from my head.
A few Risperdal will make my mind rest.
'Will save me, release me, from crushing duress!

RISPERDAL (11/17/98)
When I hear voices that don't exist,
Two things help me to deal with this:
Getting some exercise makes 'voices' stop,
And taking some Risperdal helps a lot.

Sometimes my son laughs at my wit.
When I take a Risperdal, it makes me a hit—
I'm giddy, I laugh, I'm a match for my son.
But side effects come and that is not fun*.

* (I had to stop taking Risperdal because I developed a bad reaction to it, of bad headaches when it started wearing off.)

SIDE EFFECTS (8/30/98)
I fall asleep repeatedly.
Abrupt jolts wake me up.
Risperdal helps me feel good.
But a side effect erupt.

The next day relief transforms
From rest so calm and sweet,
To a vise-like headache,
Negating past relief.

During the time that Dr. Williams has been my psychiatrist he's given me talk therapy and counseling. And I also began writing volumes of poetry. Following are some of the poems.

EBB AND FLOW MOODS (1998)
Thinking of the other person,

More than of myself.
Accepting pain, forgiving,
When someone doesn't help.

Being carefree, fun loving,
And glad to be alive.
Suddenly I run in fear.
I seek a place to hide.

I hide the hurts within my heart,
So no one else can see.
I fear I'll be rejected
If I let someone near me.

Constantly I ebb or flow.
I rise toward the sun.
Or I am drawn into vast depths
I struggle to rise from.

I hang on without answers,
I'm seeking ways to find,
Distraction from a reticent
Haunting in my mind.

    The first time I had hallucinations was when I was heavily medicated. I had visual, tactile, and auditory hallucinations as side effects of some of my psychiatric medicines.

    I heard knocks on the door when nobody was there. I heard a herd of horses run through my back yard, and a witch cackling. Someone tapped me on the back when no one was there, and once, I felt my stuffed animal's soft fur turn coarse and I saw its eyes glow a leery green. It was only a large beautiful white bunny with long floppy ears which Christy had given me.

HALLUCINATIONS (11/17/98)

I fear an evil monster.
I fear someone stalks me.
One night I feared my bunny
I slept with tenderly.

I woke to feel its fur had changed.
Its eyes, no longer plain.
I threw it down in horror.
My Bunny not the same.

No longer was it cherished.
I threw Bunny away.
But then I recalled something
I heard my doctor say—

"Get close to the thing you fear,
A little at a time.
Try to face it gradually,
And courage you will find."

I took my bunny from the trash.
Now it's back on my bed.
I licked my fear of cottontail.
Now a pillow for my head.

My children inspire me. Once, Phil went camping on the beach with Greg, little Matthew, and me. At the end of our trip, Phil gave me some small stones he had collected on the seashore. They were incredibly beautiful—smooth, and odd-shaped, in colors of white, gray, brown, yellow, orange and green.

Later, I was having a bad day. I locked myself in the bathroom where I toyed with the idea of taking my life. There, I saw on the bathroom shelf, a glass vase filled with the little multi-colored stones that Daniel had given me at the beach. Sticking out of the vase was a tiny glass balloon that Christy had given me. The sight stirred warm memories.

HATE FLEW AWAY WITH A BALLOON (7/22/98)

Yesterday I wanted to die.
I sought ways to take my life.
Yet I set down tools to hurt myself
When keepsakes calmed my strife:

From the beach were rocks Phil liked,
Sitting in a vase.
With the rocks was a glass balloon.
The sight brought a smile to my face.

I reached down to touch the glass.
It was blue and smooth and frail.
Christy picked it out for me,
Her love for me to tell.

All the rocks from at the beach
Reminded me of when
We were happy camping there.
My heart held joy again.

My thoughts of nature and of love
Brought power to go on.
Despair gave way to tender love.
The will to die . . . gone.

GLASS BALLOONS (7/27/98)

> Today my glass balloon lies in a pile of little
> sharp fragments.
> Little Matthew, if you broke my balloon—
> surely by accident,
> Get your pennies to buy me another—or maybe we
> can glue the broken glass back together.
> I can't bear to throw away the pieces.
> (I might need a glass balloon again sometime.)

My family seems to forget my angry outbursts after the moment is passed. But not when I broke the TV knob when I aimlessly threw something across the room. The broken knob was a reminder of my loss of control. I do not want to be violent or lose control. I was discouraged to the point of despair. Matthew started crying and I had trouble pulling myself back together. So I decided to protect myself and my family by putting myself to sleep for a while. I took six mild sleeping pills in my hand. I had never violated prescription directions in this way before. And I knelt at my bedside and prayed for reassurance that putting myself to sleep to protect my family was the best thing to do. I didn't want to hurt anyone or anything and I could think of no other way to protect myself and my loved ones than to put myself to sleep for a while. But praying opened my mind to an alternate idea—to call Dr. Williams, which I did instead of taking those pills. The following poem tells about that experience.

RETURN TO PEACE (1998)
I fell into a pit of despair,
Feeling mistrust. Oppression was there.
And when I was tempted to want to die,
In no one but God did my trust lie.
I asked God for guidance as I knelt in prayer.
God prompted my heart to seek Doctor's care.

Dr. Williams was free when I called him. He suggested I take a walk. I told him I couldn't because I was too tired. So he directed me to take a double dose of Risperdal, and that worked to calm me. I spent the rest of the morning holding Matt and reading him stories.

Sometimes I try to give myself therapy, as follows.

DIARY ENTRY (6/97)

Dear Beverly,

This is your mind speaking! If you lose me, here I am! Come and find me! If you want to kill yourself, that's not you. First, don't do it. Don't entertain the idea or permit yourself to think about it. It's against the rules. If a loved one drives you crazy, call Cheri McDonald fast, or a friend. Don't hold it in until you feel hopeless. Try to find peace before the day ends. When you are just blue, concentrate on music, work projects you enjoy, or do anything to get through the day with your thoughts on something that doesn't pull you down.

When you feel your head's going to fly off and you want to scream, be assured it won't happen!

Noises bother you? Talk unnerves you? Interruptions stress you almost unbearably? You'll get your break. You always do! Treasure listening to your kids talk about their interests.

Cherish their interruptions more than your time to be alone. In time, they will be grown. Love your kids now, while time lasts.
 –From Your Mind.

DIARY ENTRY (11/12/98)

Today I awoke at 5 AM and worked on this chapter on my computer. I felt sad when I read some poems I had written about hopelessness and despair. A depressed mood fell over me. At that moment six-year-old Matthew with a smile brighter than a crescent moon jumped into my bed. Matthew's ecstasy upon finding his favorite blanket under my covers, bid me an invitation to snuggle up next to him. So off went my computer and on went an overwhelming adoration for this child. Next, I was beside him as he worked at the computer trying to create a special multi-colored pumpkin. As I watched the entertainment Matt made for me on the computer screen, I reflected on the day ahead. Would it be like yesterday when I had slept in 'til 2:00 PM and was still tired? When I finally got a two-hour momentum going it ended abruptly in fatigue. "What was my life coming to?"

I remembered how yesterday, I felt like being violent, so I retreated into my bathroom and locked the door. I put on my nightgown and enclosed myself in the shower stall, with paints and brushes and wood to make some Christmas gifts—which diverted my thoughts from violence. At 7:30 PM, I retreated to a support group called, "Emotions Anonymous". There I was taught to seek God's will for me, (not my stubborn will to have strength like I used to.) I tried to accept my humble circumstances and make the most out of them. Depression comes from being hard on myself, and from forgetting the simple self-appreciation God inspires me to have.

My thoughts returned to Matthew on the computer. He printed for me a determined looking pumpkin which I taped beside my computer to remind me of my determination to appreciate the little things in life. And I decided to not type here, the depressing, hopeless poems I had earlier reviewed. Bitterness and resentment faded away. Gratitude filled my heart.

DIARY ENTRY (2/17/99)

As I finish this chapter, I am hoping to find someone who can cure my split personality parts. I heard of a new therapist named Patrick Poor. I turn to God, who I trust, to lead me where to go. For I feel I need someone professional to help me.

CONCLUSION

I have a strong will to not give up. Any self-respect or hope that I have has been strengthened by those professionals who are cheering for me I don't know how I nor my family could have survived without the help the "shrinks" gave me.

Like my neighbor Tanya who faces the ice of the rink—it would not be easy for me to face the 'ice' of life, without my coaches.

CHAPTER 5

Like A Bridge Over Troubled Waters

ONCE UPON A TIME

Enemies

A tall man and a short man harvested their orchards and gems on two sides of a river. One night, the tall man—who was jealous of the short man's gem harvest—crossed the river in a boat and knocked down the quarry's entrance, caving it all in upon itself so that there was no more opening leading into the mines. At the same time in the night, the short man—who was jealous of the tall man's fruit and nut harvest—crossed the river downstream and burned down the tall man's orchards. Soon, each man moved away, and the charred ground and caved-in mine stood idle.

Friends

Once upon a time Brother Tall and a Brother Short built their houses on opposite shores of a river. Both men had orchards and gem mines. Both men watched each other as they went about their work. Brother Tall envied how easily Brother Short fit into narrow mine openings. Brother Short envied how easily Brother Tall harvested his orchards. Soon a bridge was built across the river. Brother Tall offered to help Brother Short harvest his orchards. Brother Short offered to help collect gems from Brother Tall's gem mines. To this day their prosperity is increasing along with their friendship.

Peace Versus Fear

Moonlight illuminates a tall man crossing a bridge during the middle of the night. The tall man is pushing a cart full of produce across the bridge. He leaves it on a short man's porch as an anonymous gift. At the same time moonlight illuminates a short man crossing the bridge. He carries gasoline and matches. Jealous of his neighbor's prosperity, he destroys the very orchards which had produced his awaiting gift. Eventually the generous tall man whose orchards had been destroyed moves away. Later he dies, with a big heart and a small pocketbook. The short man, who remained behind, took over the tall man's property. Years later, he dies with a big pocketbook and a bitter heart. No one knows if the bridge is still there. The short man, suspicious of everyone, had guarded it with a gun.

I too have felt peaceful, fearful, loving, and kind at different times. I know little about securing good relationships—which is the subject of this chapter. Perhaps building bridges over troubled waters will be the best I can do.

DIARY ENTRY (12/98)

I had a darling fluffy puppy who I loved, and he loved me. He followed me all around. He had been born in my home by my Golden Retriever who mated with a Rottweiler after he jumped through a window of our home, breaking the glass, while my daughter was babysitting him. My puppy was my pick of the litter of eleven pups. But while I was on a camping trip, a loved one—who had promised to take care of my puppy until my return—gave him away to an untraceable source. I had been counting on my puppy to give protection, comfort, and reassurance in the face of my fears. Upon coming home, I happily anticipated seeing my puppy again. I had known my loved one didn't like my puppy but I had trusted leaving my puppy in my loved one's care. When I arrived home, I found out that my puppy was gone. I fell apart. "Fluffy Joe" was the name of my puppy.

FLUFFY JOE (8/31/98)
    Eyes looking up loyally.
    Your presence promised safety.
    You were devout.
    And I loved you.

    Fluffy Joe,
    You kept me from being scared.
    I trusted in you.
    Now when I'm scared, I'll miss you very badly.
    And I'll know I am alone.

FLUFFY JOE (1998)
    Who has you now?
    I miss you.
    I adored you.
    We had so many plans.

    I anticipated so many blessings
    Coming from you.
    I feel so hopeless.
    And I'm tired of trusting.

About that time I had been hearing audible hallucinations as a side effect of medication. I'd hear someone knock on the door when no one was there. My puppy had been my hope for being able to tell if the sound was in my head—or real. When I'd hear a knock, I'd look at Fluffy Joe's ears and if they were lifted up, then I knew he heard it too, and I'd go answer the door.

I felt hurt when Fluffy Joe was given away, and I had trouble handling all the hurt I felt.

It's challenging to get along with people. Yet, I don't want to give the idea that there are not beautiful, enduring relationships of love in my life. Part of my problems come from my past.

When I was 11 years old, I suffered a mass peer rejection where every friend I had at school—even my best friend who I called on the phone after school—refused to talk to me. I attempted suicide for the first time that day because I thought I was rejected due to some innate "badness," and I could think of no way to make things better.

Trauma from the past still affects me in the present. Subconsciously, my past alienation is still going on. Yet, when I live in the moment—which is hard sometimes—but if I try to cherish the moment, I often realize there is much love to be appreciated.

Once a woman came to my home to buy a little hamster from my daughter. I let the woman in our front door and noticed that she stood there sweeping the room with her eyes, seeing my children playing—with toys, art projects, books, food, and homework spread across the room. I started to apologize for the mess, but the woman said, "Your home is beautiful!" Then, when she saw the perplexed look on my face, she added, "I mean the feeling here is beautiful." And I had to agree.

HOPE (2/5/99)
>Vulnerable sometimes,
>I get knocked off my feet.
>But lifted up by kindness,
>I rise above defeat.
>
>Both trusting, and untrusting,
>I try to hold to love—
>For other people and myself.
>That's what my hope's made of.

DIARY ENTRY (2/99)

I have a six-year-old named Matthew. When I despair and believe others would be happy without me around, I think of my six-year-old. No one could give him my special love. I fear for his welfare, should I be gone. I always choose to hang on—even when nearly every fiber of my being craves to die. He is like a bridge over troubled waters for me.

DIARY ENTRY (10/19/98)

Last month I was afraid I could resist suicide no longer. I decided I had to get away to protect myself. I prayerfully pondered where to go. I had thought of visiting my younger brother's house or my best friend's home. Then I thought of my best friend's dad 'Uncle Joe'. He is a good man who raised five children alone who were all close to my age, and who taught me how to sing and play the guitar. He lived alone in the same home I spent half of my adolescence in. He welcomed me with open arms as portrayed in the following poem.

REPRIEVE (10/19/98)

Tired of life,
I pack my bags and leave.
My childhood retreat bid me to pay a visit.
I savor its sweet nostalgia as I pull up the street.

I cherish memories of names etched with marbles
in the cement walkway,
Of sitting on the front steps for hours talking,
growing close,
Of countless late night walks (or runs) around
the block.
To my delight the furnishings, the old woven rug,
And the six-foot llama hanging were still there.
I'm glad there are holes in the carpet in the stairs.
It reminds me that it is the same carpet I walked up
During the happiest days of my childhood.
Even the phone is the same old one.

The rooms, the sights, the smells, all take me back
thirty years,
As did Uncle Joe's farm cooking, and memories of
backyard produce and parties.
The guitars still sit anxious for animation by young
and old hands.
There I awake and retire to the sound of Uncle Joe
playing his guitar.

So carefree. So free.
So much love and comfort.
Uncle Joe, the sole survivor of his homestead,
had not changed.

We shared late night movies, bared secrets,
and sang funny songs,
A mutual buoying up.

He loved me, accepted me, listened to me, honored me,
and built me up generously.
Alone one afternoon, sitting on his front steps,
I read a piece of his mail, a religious magazine.
As I read, God held me in his hand and let the suicidal
thoughts and hopelessness drain out of me.
Refreshed now, I go home.

I'd love to fill my home with peace, like Uncle
Joe's home.
Then it would be a refuge for weary ones who
need a pick up.
God, let me sleep. Its strength renews my efforts.
But if fatigue reigns, let my heart still be kind.

I love friends with whom you can be yourself and know that you are accepted. I'll never forget that when I came out of my stay in the mental hospital and came to a family gathering, my husband's younger brother saw me and came up to me. He spoke not a word. He just put his arms around me and comforted me. To understand, and be understood, is a bridge over troubled waters.

CHAPTER 6

Poisoned Birds And Bees

The following poem introduces this chapter's journey from innocence into confusion, and then back into the light.

> POISONED BIRDS AND BEES (2/7/99)
> Poisoned birds and bees?
> Confusion over sex?
> Could it be a child's abuse?
> Can toxins young minds vex?
>
> A boil or a cancer
> Beneath the surface lies.
> Although the child can't see it there,
> He's crippled. He can't rise.
>
> But when he sees the cancer,
> Or sees the boil sore,
> No matter how he cleans it out,
> It seems there's always more.
>
> He's grateful when it's finally healed!
> No blindness clouds his mind.
> Joy replaces guilt.
> He's glad for a long time!

BLINDED

When I was around twelve, I was sought out by a relative who was a role model in some ways—but who had also become engrossed in deception which led him to molest me. I then felt a most tumultuous battle inside. Simultaneously, I didn't want to displease him, for he was an authority figure I had been taught to respect unconditionally. Yet I was stuck in conflict. Innately my heart knew something was wrong but I had long since learned to place my own feelings second to the feelings of others. Torn between my heart saying, "No", and my fear to disobey, I lost my sense of safety, my sense of self. Something changed inside of me. There was a part of me which was sweet, tender, and innocent. But a new part came out which felt incredible guilt and shame. The sweet, tender part of me just wanted, needed, to be able to trust and to be loved and cared about. But how was I to feel about trust? That my molester was trustworthy and I should disregard my conscience? Or that I couldn't trust leaders or people who become close to me?

In time the molester was stopped and was threatened severely. His attention towards me stopped very abruptly including all the non-abusive attention he had given me. It seemed as if I had become invisible and didn't exist anymore. I learned that a "worse than death" ultimatum had been given to him because of his involvement with me. I believed that if the ultimatum had happened to him, it would have been my fault. At that heart-wrenching moment I acquired a belief that femininity was bad, that I was wicked, and that if a man ever came close to me again his life would be destroyed. The sweet, innocent part of me was shut down by feelings of badness. I learned to not trust—to not trust adults or leaders, to not trust in myself, to not trust in security, to not trust in love.

FEELINGS DISHONORED
>
> Getting double messages—
> Am I loved, or am I dross?
> I dare not to defend myself.
> Silenced at all cost.
> I have feelings but it seems
> My feelings don't exist.
> How can I speak what I feel
> When my feelings folks resist?

SIGHT

Late, on New Year's Eve 1988, while my husband and children were playing table games in the family room, I was pouring out my heart to God in the privacy of my room. For a year I had been looking at the subconscious self-loathing which had come to the surface when I had my emotional breakdown two years earlier. Dr. Chevy would not let me sweep my guilty feelings under the carpet. Nor would my counselor Gary Golden—who I had met with weekly the year before. Gary had pointed out that I habitually denied how I felt because I thought I was bad if I didn't "feel" the way I thought I was supposed to feel. Gary said I could not learn and grow until I accepted my feelings compassionately—not accusingly. Eventually I felt attraction to Gary, so I quit therapy with him and entered a dark period of my life. For a year, I laboriously put one foot in front of the other.

Although these months were the darkest of my life, I had some of my most uplifting spiritual experiences during this time. That New Year's Eve, I was pondering how I had never accepted being intimate without guilt and shame. I had habitually asked my husband Greg if he still loved me following intimacy, and I couldn't believe I wouldn't be rejected and despised by him at any moment. But when I prayed that New Year's Eve, I asked for a miracle. I'd looked at my guilt about intimacy from every angle. I'd struggled in my mind for a year with conflicting thoughts. Logically, sex made sense, but in my heart I was still weighed down with guilt. I'd done all I could to heal my feelings, but nothing worked. In tearful humility, I knelt down and asked God for a change of heart. I won't describe my prayer, for it was too sacred. But with all my heart and every ounce of faith I possessed, I sought to be a woman unashamed, grateful for her femininity, cherishing her femininity.* I thought of a pure, perfect mother in heaven, and imagined a beam of healing light coming from above, and entering my mind, and transforming me to feel accepting of myself, and my prayer was answered. I still stand in awe—even many years later—over how God blessed me that night. My gratitude to Him for changing my heart is no less now than it was on that New Year's Eve—the eve of a new heart.

*(Imagining what I longed for, while in a deeply meditative state, was inspired by my reading of "Eliminate Your S D B's (Self-Defeating Behaviors)" by Jonathan M. Chamberlain.)

NO MORE BLIND
    A chaste life in deed,
    But tainted in mind.
    The rapture of marriage
    Could not fully shine—

    In shame and in silence
    I marveled that he
    Could show me affection
    When I felt so guilty.

I struggled so hard,
To accept my feelings.
Nurturing love
And hope led to healings.

After my heart
Was renewed by God's power,
I seemed to enjoy
Being me every hour.

Like blind souls who see,
And forever are glad,
It's great to feel guiltless
Over feelings I have.

A few years ago at Venice Beach while Greg and I played, I decided to increase the good character traits of Little b in regards to my feelings about intimacy. Then I decided to likewise increase the good character traits of Liz and of my other personalities in regards to intimacy. These simple poems are some of the poems written at that time to express joy, where there once had been guilt.

HAPPY (1997)
I am not sad.
For I was Little b.
No guile, no sin,
No guilt in she.

A joy just to live!
Simple, genuine.
Relishing, seeking,
All that seems fine.

Appreciation
Flows out like a spring.
A heart full of love—
So much joy it can bring!

PEACE (1997)
Liz isn't perfect.
But she's mature.
Her feelings she shared
With Greg for sure.

Effects from drugs
She must endure.*
Still, in Greg's love,
She is secure.

Guilt and badness,
Blaming herself.
Calling on God,
His mercy she felt.

Don't worry, Liz.
Love makes it right,
Holy, and pure.
Sweet peace this night.

* (Medicines for mental illness sometimes lessen normal sexual feelings.)

AT THE BEACH (1997)
Pacita's desire
Is matched by his own.
Frolicking, teasing,
Such fun to be known.

Losing herself,
She thinks first of him.
Therein her life
Is peace-filled again.

SINCERE (1997)

Lisa's as loving
As loving can be.
Walls tumble down
With thoughts shared freely.

She feels less delight
Than she felt before.
No mind. She is happy
To please and adore.

REBECCAH (1997)

Thinking of him
Unselfishly,
Puts her heart
Where it wants to be.

The joy she finds
Surpasses her dreams.
Tranquil and happy,
Her glad heart sings.

LEAH (1997)

Joy beyond measure,
Our love to treasure.
Why do I ache
For a retake?

I'll say how I feel,
Sincere, frank, and real.
My heart wants to give—
That's the reason I live!

JAMIE (1997)
Like Rebeccah, Jamie's herself.
Play and wonder pulled off the shelf.
Tiring from the effects of meds,
Still appreciation's in her head.

More recently I wrote the following to express my joy over intimacy with my husband.

DEAR GREG (1999)
A few nights back I left a note
For when you went to bed.
It asked you hug and hold me—
But no memory's in my head!

Then last night I postponed my meds
So I could be awake.
Now I recall everything!
I hope there'll be retakes!

Too sacred to write, I thank God and you
For such brilliant firework shows!
Beyond earth we soared. Without limits we flew.
How I cherish these bonds that we know!

CHAPTER 7

Rain Makes The Flowers Grow

DIARY ENTRY (1/99)

I planted sweet alyssum, dianthus, and green onions in a long flower pot on our front porch. December in California has been good to the seeds which raised their heads within a week. If we were to put as much work into growing flowers as we have put into our marriage, the whole world would be in bloom.

RAIN MAKES THE FLOWERS GROW (2/18/99)

Rain killed my pink heaven's breath.
It rained too hard, too fast.
The tender growth and beauty
Left sorrow as it passed.

Yet other flowers flourish,
Sown in a safer spot.
When rain falls down on them,
They grow and bloom a lot.

I think of rain as hard times,
That we in marriage know.
The pain and work and struggle
Can sometimes make love grow.

One big part of the love between my husband and me is from our shared love for our children. We believe that one of the best gifts we can give our children is to show them that we love each other.

EARTH AND SKY (2/18/99)
    If Earth were Mom,
    Sky would be Dad.
    He'd help blow the sails
    And kites that kids have.

    And when kids get sleepy
    And want to come home,
    Mom's there to hold them
    'Til next time they roam.

    And when the kids savor
    What makes them feel neat,
    They'll think of the sunset—
    Where Earth and Sky meet.

PRINCESS

Once there was a lovely princess who was locked in a stifling tower by a dark monster. Near her castle lived a knight in shining armor who was an idealist with his feet on the ground and his head in the clouds.

One day the princess escaped the stifling tower and forgot the monster, (except for when she had nightmares.) It was then that the knight in shining armor discovered her, and they fell in love. As they frolicked around the castle grounds together, it seemed no one could be happier. But soon the knight had to go supervise the laying of a city wall and the structural plans for newer and bigger and better castles. So the princess, who missed the knight, gardened, went to market, studied in the library, decorated the castle, and taught the village children how to read and write. One day the knight and princess found they had seven beautiful children running 'round about their feet and all over the castle grounds. As their children grew, the daring princess let them cross streams on slippery rocks, and climb up some sides of the castle which she thought they had good footing on, in spite of the knight's caution. The princess thought life was all play. Even work was fun. The children worked daily and faithfully in the kitchen, the garden, grooming horses, running errands, cross country hiking, and studying the princess's favorite literary works.

The knight spent long hours away working on improving the city. One of the princess's main problems was that when her knight came home late, he dismissed the children from their bedtime routine for a free-play time with Dad. The princess felt frustrated, but she said nothing. She waited far past her bedtime to go through the children's routine all over again after the knight was finished playing with them. She silently tried to follow the knight's lead. However, conflicting emotions and fears led her to sink in sadness and withdraw from her knight for a season. She felt ashamed for disagreeing with her knight—like she felt ashamed and fearful while a captive of the dark monster. Once she withdrew from the entire kingdom for a long time. Her mind sank and she felt bound by cords which she didn't know how to unbind. So the knight carried a heavier load than usual on his shoulders and cared for the children alone when the princess was sick. He nurtured the princess with unconditional love until she recovered.

With recovery, many wonderful things happened in the lives of the princess and the children. Their daily trips to the country were full of laughter, play, and happiness! The knight was happy too! The princess only forgot her happiness when she remembered the dark monster. Then she believed that no matter how happy she was, in the end, the monster would catch her and consign her to an eternity of dark, stifling, wretchedness. She even feared for the children. Confused by fear, she chastised them when all they needed was encouragement. She burdened her knight with her complaints. The knight, at the same time, began asking that the princess carry out regulations with the children that she did not agree with. She obeyed resentfully—for she had learned from the dark monster to never argue. Concealing her own opinions, she harbored anger, and then self-condemnation, for she had been taught long ago that it was wrong to feel anger, and that it was also wrong to disagree with anybody. During good seasons, when the princess broke away from her self-condemnation, her confidence in herself and in her children grew. She fostered closeness. She asked for respect. She respected her knight. Yet, sometimes, when he was gone, she changed his rules. Her knight would return and invalidate her laws if he disagreed. The princess grew sick and weary. Then strong and assertive. Sometimes she led the children in big ways, while the knight watched silently in the distance. Other times she collapsed in hopelessness and silently watched in the background as her knight enthusiastically raised the children in his own way. In spite of the lack of unity between the princess and the knight, their love burned bright. She forgave him, and he forgave her. Though for a long time, neither forgot the other's weakness. The princess was cautious in supporting the knight's leadership. And the knight did not always trust the princess's judgment.

The princess' family is my family. And I am the princess.

The knight is my husband, Greg. We are still evolving. Recently, (January 1999), while living in a homeless shelter to protect my family from myself, and to give myself a rest from stress, I read a book on marriage by Helen Andelin called "Fascinating Womanhood". The book said that a man wants to be accepted and admired by his wife more than anything. It pointed out ways a woman could express herself more honestly and more effectively. I returned home to live with my family the day I finished Andelin's book. I tried to replace critique with acceptance and appreciation. My knight immediately noticed a change in me. He made me feel more beautiful and loved than ever! I'm trying to make our time together my highest priority. My knight is happier, and so am I.

STORMS AND NEW GROWTH

I brought into my marriage my love and devotion and twenty years of previous experiences in life. These experiences have made me overall the good person that I am. But sometimes past storms that I have not fully recovered from, complicate my marriage. Certainly having multiple personality disorder has made my marriage more difficult.

One night I wore myself out trying to cook dinner. I asked Greg to clean up after me, which he did. He saran wrapped & put away everything except the sliced onions. When I walked back in the room, and saw the onions, I made a split-second judgment that he had left the onions out to spite me, because he doesn't likes onions and I do. And in a split-second, I had thrown the plate of onions out the window, shattering shards of glass from the biggest window in our house, into our backyard pool. With instant regret, and suicidal urges, I ran out of the house barefoot in the night before things could get worse.

ONIONS (7/16/98)

Yesterday my mood became
An enemy to me.
Instead of deeming Greg a friend,
He seemed an enemy.

He left the onions sitting out,
That I sliced the night before—
I thought that he had left them out
To spite my mind so sore.

I felt fearful, undermined,
Not heard, not understood.
I sensed he loathed me. But logic said:
My mind was not too good.

I broke the window unaware
I'd 'crack' for I didn't see,
Subconsciously I felt as though
He was oppressing me.

I have not since broke windows,
I just run away.
I wish that I could find more peace.
I yearn to see that day.

HOPE

When I criticized my husband while talking to my therapist, she told me to lower my expectations of Greg. I privately made a list: "What I will not expect Greg to do". It worked for half a day. Then I made a list of what I knew Greg could be trusted to do. Since then, although I get exasperated sometimes with our differences, I have more hope. My weakness was in picking on Greg's faults, instead of focusing on his love.

MARRIAGE BLUES

In 1981, after our fourth child was born, I fell out of love with Greg for a year, and Greg felt that he was married to a witch and that he'd be miserable forever! Our dormant love was revived when Greg was asked to teach a Sunday School class on family relations. He started reading a lot of books on marriage and relationships. As a result of what he read, he decided to make a special effort to appreciate me and build me up.

IT WAS MAGIC (1996)

I became grouchy,
'Suppressed anger in store.
Much of our love
Had gone out the door.

I felt very hostile.
My cruel words had bite.
Then he did something
That made my heart light.

Very sincerely,
Heart-meltingly, too,
He praised little things
That he'd see me do.

I'd be doing the dishes,
And he'd touch me soft.
For my work and child care
He'd thank me a lot!

My anger drained out,
My perspective turned 'round,
As day after day,
Appreciation he'd sound.

It's been sixteen years,
But I'll never forget
The kindness which made
My sweetheart a hit!

LOVE NOTES (12/96)
Notes my husband gives me
Make me think he's neat!
He says he likes my smile,
And tells me I am sweet.

He sees me with the children,
'Says, "Thanks for what you do."
He thanks me for my friendship,
And tells me, "I love you."

The following poems depict the 'showers' and 'flowers' of marriage.

THE 'GIRLISH' PART (2/99)
This week a stage friend asked me
Why my acting ceased.*
"It hasn't. I've a husband.
When we differ, I keep peace.

If he hurts me, I say so,
No feelings are held in.
A pout, a spunk, in child-like truth,
Tears wet my quivering chin.

I'm learning to let feelings speak
With inner worth, and calm.
(In past days I'd get mad and yell,
Or silently walk on.)

Now, accepting both of us,
There's less room for complaint.
He responds to words of love.
I won't humiliate.

Acting on the stage is great!
But marriage is more fun!
When I play the 'girlish' part,
His honor I have won."

* (While raising my family, I've been in small town productions of the Music Man, Cinderella, and other local theatrical performances with some of my children.)

A HOME THAT'S KIND AND WARM (1994)
To Greg I seem more beautiful
And bear a brighter sheen,
From having a sweet spirit,
Than from keeping the house clean.

Which comforts me, as once again,
The housework lacks success.
Low in strength, I seek God's help,
And find peace, in this mess.

For just as Christ was welcomed
Into a humble barn,
If God is near and love is there,
Our home is kind and warm.

OUR FRIDAY NIGHT DATE (5/13/97)

I was mad at the kids,
Discouraged, too!
It was our date night.
But what good could it do?

I decided to go,
For I knew it would bar
A big outburst,
So I got in the car.

Down the freeway,
In just four miles,
A transformation
Revived my smiles.

I laid my load
Of problems aside.
Too tired to solve them,
I enjoyed the ride.

We played air hockey,
Took walks—not a few.
We browsed in the bookstore,
And gallery, too.

I felt Greg's love.
He listened and cared.
His talk—entertaining,
Much laughter we shared.

He made me feel better.
Now that our date's through,
I can hardly believe
How much better my view!

OPENING DOORS (10/13/93)

Struggling in marriage,
I knelt down in prayer.
No answer came.
Couldn't help be somewhere?

Then came a friend,
Who'd struggled before.
Discouraged, she thought
Her divorce was in store.

Then she had a thought
Which opened a door:
'Twas improving herself,
And loving him more.

My friend's marriage lives!
Their home is so warm.
Though they have difference,
They've respect, not scorn.

Now my criticizing
And blaming I see
Are blocking the way,
And hurting me.

We two may differ.
But I'll love, not control.
Through prayer and goodwill,
I'll change me, and grow.

THE CYCLE (1997)

Yesterday I marveled
At the strong love which we felt.
Like school kids bathed in stardust,
One mere look and I would melt.

Gratitude for Greg
Soared right off the scale!
Everything he did,
I enjoyed so well.

We marveled at our happiness—
Effortless it seemed!
Then there rose up tension,
Which fear and mistrust bring.

What makes the bliss come to an end?
It seems it's here to stay
Until I'm struggling to be kind,
In vain through night and day.

I wish that this cycle,
Would not repeat itself.
But I've known it all my life.
Dear Lord, I need thy help.

Whether I keep giving love,
Or just endure in pain,
I pray each time I sink,
I will come up again.

APPRECIATION AND HONOR (12/10/87)

There's a loving look in your eyes
I've never seen before.
Your happiness seems deep.
Your smile uplifts me more.

You helped me with the children.
The care you give to them,
Helps us feel protected,
And comforted again.

I'd like to know you better,
Not change, or nag, or judge.
Acceptance brings me peace.
Mercy brings me love.

I trust you and you grow more.
I thank you and you're glad.
You have never cut me down,
Though chances you have had.

THANKFUL (2/20/99)

I love each night at bedtime
When you put your hand in mine.
You pray that God will bless our love
And help us to be kind.

I love it when you're sleeping
And I whisper in your ear:
"I love you so much, darling!"
And then you draw me near.

Every day when you come home
My feelings are sublime.
Every day I feel so glad
When we have a little time.

You turn the stove down where I cook,
And take me by the hand.
"Our marriage is more important!"
We both understand.

You lead me to the front yard
And we pick which way we go.
The fresh air is uplifting.
The evening sky aglow.

Our Friday dates can't be the same,
As in days of yore.
I'm tucked in bed at seven.
Less late nights than before.

So you take off from work at three!
I love what happens then!
We laugh and play and talk and learn,
And fall in love again.

CHAPTER 8

The Sun Shining Through The Clouds

I seem to be closest to God when I am in pain and I turn to Him for help. God has lighted my path, one step at a time, so I can walk through the dark. And sometimes when I cannot walk, I collapse in God's arms and He carries me into the light, as a loving Father carries a child.

The following poems show how God's light breaks through the clouds of my life, bringing peace and hope and comfort.

LORD, I'VE GONE CRAZY (1996)
>   Lord, I've gone crazy
>   And you know it's so!
>   Yet you have been with me
>   Wherever I go.
>
>   My family, my joy,
>   I try to serve well.
>   But all I can do
>   Is to spare them my hell.
>
>   I keep running away,
>   To escape awful strife.
>   I can't even drive,
>   Or I'll end my own life.

But through all this pain,
There's a light I can see.
There's a warmth I can feel,
From thy arms around me.

STRENGTH/BURNOUT (1996)
Sometimes I pray and find strength to go.
Sometimes God whispers,
"You're tired, go slow."
Often an outburst or suicide plan
Follow attempts to do more than I can.

Sometimes I'm strong for over a week,
Pulling off projects, efficient and sleek.
Sometimes I can't plan one moment of time.
Then God whispers, "Rest, to yourself be kind."

TRYING (12/13/96)
I tell God I'm confused,
'Don't know which way to go.
God tells me, "Trying's good enough."
He says, "I love you so."

SOLITUDE (2/14/95)
My heart embraces the beauty
Of a quiet cloudy night.
'God's way of saying, "I love you.
Everything will be all right."

REASSURANCE (4/4/97)
Sometimes I feel so lowly,
I cry, "God, am I in tune?
I feel like such a failure.
Have I brought on this gloom?"

"My child, I love and hear you.
You're weak, and you're not Home yet.
But you're trying, and still moving onward.
Your reward you surely will get."

Once I tried with exasperation to get my heart to open up and share with Greg. But my heart was sealed by fear. Later, at a place of worship where I felt safe and validated by God, my anxiety let up. There I opened up and was able to share with Greg.

A HOLY PLACE (1997)
In a holy place came comfort
And strength for days to come.
With Greg I reached inside my heart
To share things I once shunned.

He understood. I understood.
It couldn't have been elsewhere,
But in the safety of God's peace,
That I found strength to share.

I AM A WARRIOR (6/10/98)
The choice of suicide tempts me again.
In stress, in sadness, and in my heart's pain.
But I realize now where this urge comes from,
Someone who wants my life to be done!

It's not all in my head, nor past my control.
There's a war against good! And Satan's the foe!
He sees where I'm weak and where I'm off guard.
Now, seeing his ploy, choosing good is less hard.
Less pity for self. Less thoughts are turned in.
I'll fight! I am mad! And I feel I will win!

NOT ALONE (11/24/96-written one year to the day after I had been admitted to the Mental Hospital)

Who knows that today,
One year ago,
I was down
So very low?

Once more I'm alone,
In sadness again.
No one but God
Could know where I've been.

I always need God,
And He's always there.
Each ache of loneliness,
Eased by a prayer.

I'll just kneel down,
And pour out my heart.
Where man's help ends,
God's help starts.

TRYING TO REMEMBER WHAT IT FEELS LIKE TO BE NICE (5/10/98)

I didn't accuse, mistrust, or blame,
For almost thirteen days.
It seemed so effortless back then.
God, revive my kind ways!

I bit my tongue. I gave a smile.
I thought of others first.
My goal to be of service
Filled my heart and quenched my thirst.

Perhaps, I'll just give love to me!
I'll take a break to read,
Or write, or sing, or take a walk.
Fresh air feels good to breathe!

I think I've found my answer—
My mind had run away!
I'll just slow down and rest in peace
For what's left of today.

THE ANSWER (1996)

Feeling awful sadness,
Deep, deep in my soul,
Unable to bear it,
I didn't know where to go.

What was the solution
To get past all this pain?
What could be the answer?
I turned to God again.

God answered me the next day
While I sat in church.
My daughter said the choir
Seemed one of the worst.

Yet I couldn't tell the difference
If heavenly angels sang.
The songs and words of heaven
Brought hope to me again.

The children sang "I Wonder
When Jesus Comes Again."
And then I knew within my soul
I'd bear my pain 'til then.

No magic cure to bring relief
But in my mind I saw
Myself with all the children,
Approach the Lord in awe.

His loving eyes would see me.
Perhaps he'd hold me tight.
My heart knew from that moment,
Everything would be all right.

And then another answer came
To turn me to my brothers:
"Your sadness will be lifted,
As you share love with others."

THE ANSWER, AGAIN (2/13/97)
God, so gracious, tells me
The answer, sweet, once more:
"Your pains won't all be lifted,
But through service, they'll be less sore.

SUICIDE (2/14/99)
"You'll never kill yourself," they say.
"You would not make that choice."
But when depressed souls take their lives,
Don't judge. Please hold your voice!

The act seen by a knowing
God May be beyond control.
Why do brains exhaust and fail?
Only God can know.

I fear not judgment if I die.
I know God understands.
In life I give God all my love.
In death I'm in his hands.

You must not judge that someone
Should have given more.
Perhaps they've given all they had.
God's mercy calls the score.

IF YOU ARE STRUGGLING (12/98)
Worn down by life,
Crushed and abrased.
Though bent down in darkness,
In light we'll be raised.

Though we are struggling,
Without a quick cure.
It will not last.
Of this I am sure.

Kindness can heal us.
But it will take time.
Ill will impedes us.
Love helps us climb.

EPILOGUE

My Ferris Wheel Ride Is Over

RECOVERY
(Written in 2000)

By 1999, my multiple personality disorder became so life-threatening that I daily faced a likelihood of committing suicide on impulse. I wanted more help than my psychiatrist knew how to offer. I felt I needed to find a cure for my split personality or I would lose my life. I searched the phone book and called local therapists to inquire if any knew how to heal a split personality, to no avail. I felt desperate, and prayed with all my heart to find somebody to help me. It was the biggest fight of my life—to stay alive—and I prayed harder than I have ever prayed before—or since. I felt I needed someone professional to guide me, but I didn't know where to look.

Then I visited my friend Dean who was recovering from a diabetic coma. It was February of 1999. I wasn't living at home at the time. I had wanted to protect myself and my family after a suicide attempt and an explosive outburst where I blindly threw something that accidentally bruised little Matthew's chest, so I had moved into a homeless shelter. It was during the day, while the shelter was closed, that I visited Dean and talked to his caregiver Susan Matthews. Susan heard me tell Dean about my problems and after I returned home, she called me on the phone. "I want to share something with you that I think you'll be interested in," she said.

When Susan came to my home, I worked on a jigsaw puzzle while she spoke so I wouldn't have to get restless from whatever she said. When she told me her sister had multiple personality disorder and was healed by an intern therapist who used hypnotic therapy I was leery. She made it sound so simple, so elementary. I did not believe that such a big problem could be healed by the kind of simplicity she described. I wouldn't have considered seeing the therapist Patrick Poor—who was not even licensed yet—still in training—but I was desperate enough for help to at least pray about it. After my prayer, I knew in my heart I should at least call Patrick. After the phone call, I knew in my heart that I needed to make at least one appointment with him. During that first appointment, he gained my faith and trust.

During our first visit he helped my traumatized subconscious memories convert their stories to non-stressful memories. I was freed from so much pain after that first visit that I wasn't afraid. I crossed a bridge without hypnotically focusing my mind on the other side to keep myself from jumping off. It was night time. I was in Newhall, California taking a walk while Greg accompanied our son Sam to a drug recovery class. I stood in the middle of the bridge and stared at the moon's reflection in the water. I felt like a new person. I have since been safe from violent impulses.* I saw Patrick Poor for about one month—until he and I both agreed together that I needed no more therapy.**

* (Since 2000, I had one outburst where I slugged the hard, box-shaped television set and sprained my wrist.)

** (Since 2000, I've discovered that I have to live with occasional relapses with my split personality, or trauma disorder. But it's not as bad as before, and I know how to heal it each new time.)

Following is something I wrote in my diary when I went to Hawaii for my twenty-fifth wedding anniversary, shortly after my recovery from multiple personality disorder.

KAUA'I (5/5/99)

I feel joy like I've never felt before! Yesterday, at Kalalau Lookout, I sat above a 4,000 foot drop off to the sea. I savored the lush, green cliffs hovering over a jewel-like ocean for hours. Jumping off the edge was far from my mind.

I'm different than I was before. I'm much happier now.

MY FERRIS WHEEL RIDE IS OVER (11/26/99)

My Ferris wheel ride is over.
I'm not a 'flake' anymore.
Multiple personality disorder
Has gone right out the door.

The old gray mare seems younger.
Folks say I have a 'glow'.
My heart holds peace and love
Everywhere I go.

God's my only 'shrink' now,
In the 'rink of life*.
I pray for answers and hold God's hand.
I'm walking more upright.

Relationships are sweeter.
I never 'run away'.**
Although I've got a lot to learn
I at least can say:

I feel more love for others.
I sense that folks love me.
Walking a bridge of compassion,
Stormy waters I do not see.

The birds and bees are better.
My marriage has more peace.
My heart rests in the hands of God.
From mental illness, I'm released.

* (10/01 update–I began marriage counseling nearly a year ago and continue it, as needed. My counselors are professionals, clergymen, and friends.)

** (Postscript: 1/2019 I have left home from time to time to enjoy the solitude found in nature, but I don't call it running away. My vacations to beautiful places empower me to be able to sufficiently deal with depression and repressed anger. Between March and June 1999, I gradually weaned myself off of my psychiatric medications, and have not since used any.)

LOOKING BACK (12/8/00)

Now that I have found healing for my former multiple personality disorder for almost two years I would like to look back with hindsight. The terminology keeps changing from "split" to "multiple" to "disassociated" personality or "dissociative identity disorder." They all have to do with the same human condition of carrying unhealed wounds largely in one's subconscious mind.

My Morgan Welsh Pony, Gummi Bear, recently had a stone in her foot that was wedged in quite deeply. It had been there for a couple of days. At first her hoof appeared to have a normal cake up of dirt in it. But as I began to remove the dirt with my pick, it hit something hard. Sure enough, embedded deeply was a stone in the soft part of her foot. It would not budge as I pried at it. Finally, I pried the pick to the side of the stone and gave it one more yank. The stone went flying!

Gummi Bear had not been limping noticeably before I removed the stone, but after it was removed she limped for a few minutes. I found it interesting that she could walk normally with a stone in her foot, but when the stone was removed, it took some getting used to. I guess multiple personalities are like that. As long as no one tries to oust them, things may seem fine. But once somebody tries to get down to the tender part of one's heart, (or one's hoof), and free it of foreign matter, it can be quite a job! Especially if the foreign matter is embedded in the flesh.

Living life is like being a horse—whose hooves get dirt in them every day. It can be a problem if the dirt is full of bacteria and the horse is not in a clean place. Sharp gravel or stones can injure the hoof—as sharp words can the heart. My multiple personalities were not much different than a horse's hoof with an infection in it or with a few stones in it. After being treated, these conditions are not a problem anymore. Only in cases where hearts or hooves are not safe—where one must run on gravel all the time or live in a dirty infested stall will there be a problem. As I'm learning how to clean the grooves of Gummi Bear's hooves of foreign debris, I'm also learning to do the same for my heart on an ongoing basis—to heal wounds that are concealed. I've also learned that all hooves and hearts have their own contours, only seen from a humble view. I could not have learned how to clean the tender grooves of Gummi Bear's hooves without guidance from my Horse Whisperer friend, Julie. Also, I could not have known how to look in the subconscious part of my mind without help from Patrick Poor, and from God. I am very grateful to God for answering my prayer and letting me find healing for my split personality. Life holds more joy. I can rise above my present problems enough to see steady growth and an increase of love day by day.

DENOUEMENT

By Beverly Ann Needham
November 14, 2018

Denouement is a French word meaning "the outcome of a situation" or the "final part of a story where the pieces come together."

In this Denouement, I share diary entries in order to draw a line from 1999 to the present time. My aim is to show that I still struggle, but that I handle it in more natural ways.

October 6, 2018
Diary Entry Kentucky

I take a deep breath. Then exhale. I'm camping alone in my hippie van in Kentucky. Here I lie, under sheltering trees, looking at my van's ceiling. This 27-year-old van has wallpaper on the ceiling, with flaming suns, crescent moons, and thousands of yellow stars. Surrounded by nine huge windows, I feel like I'm in a glass house, watching the pussy-willow trees blow in the wind, and the clouds float by.

I call my car a hippie van because it symbolizes the peace I long for. Plus, I've been called Flower Child because I like to wear long dresses, with flowers in my hair. But I don't use hallucinogenic drugs or rebel against conventional values. I only rebel against my old way of thinking that others have to tell me what to do. I refuse to listen to medical doctors who suggest I take psychiatric drugs when they can't figure out what causes the aches and pains in my body. My husband Greg told one doctor, "When Beverly takes psychiatric medications, she is more prone to be violent and suicidal." That doctor replied, "I still think she should take them!" I haven't gone to that doctor since.

My former shrink from the 1990's, Doctor Williams—who medicated me more heavily than any other sincere patient he had back then—said that I didn't need medication anymore after seeing Pat Poor. "Your bipolar symptoms," Dr. Williams said, "are now just cute, bubbly and enthusiastic."

As for my down times, people usually don't know when I'm struggling. I just take off in my hippie van and let solitude, and the peace of nature heal me. Greg offers to buy me a new van, but I prefer this old one.

I recall my last night with Greg before I left for this vacation to Kentucky. I laughed as Greg told jokes about old cars breaking down. Then I reminded him of how much fun I had when my van broke down in the California Redwoods, extending my vacation in a lovely place where the wild berries grew so abundant that my pee turned purple. Then, while waiting for my van to get fixed, I ran into a friend that I hadn't seen for 40 years—a woman who had given me the first handmade quilt she ever made—as a gift for my newborn sons, Tim and Sam.

Life is an adventure, and I do not fear taking my 27-year-old van on the road. Especially to visit my daughter Butterfly in Kentucky. Here, I'm enraptured by the peace of the woods, wildlife, farmland, and flowing waters. While camping, I read books for uplift and rejuvenation. I just read about a woman who was separated from her family for 30 years after she was exported by militant radicals, and her village burned. I read about the woman's grief and how she bore the pain of her loss through giving loving service to others. Helping others lifts my pains as well.

Here, in Kentucky, I've helped my daughter Butterfly and my son-in-law Dragonfly by taking their children to school and music lessons while Dragonfly recovers from a motorcycle accident. Now, as I watch the pussy willow tree dance in the wind, I dream of spending my winter here, in Kentucky. However, Butterfly doesn't share my dream. "Mom," she says, "I don't want you to stay in Kentucky forever!"

She has a love-hate attitude toward me because of all she went through as a teenager of a mentally ill mom. I didn't protect her as she grew up. My medications made me swagger like a drunk and she was embarrassed to have her friends over. She wanted me to be there for her. But I wasn't. She survived by convincing herself that she didn't need me. Now, she is still afraid to get close to me, thinking she might lose me again.

Some people push me away. Others gravitate to me. Once, mental illness branded me. Now, I try to move past the labels. I prefer to build bridges of love to put us on common ground. I prefer to envision a light at the end of our tunnels. I don't always see my light, yet I know it will come. I've been through enough struggles to know I can make it through anything.

Recently, an old friend of mine committed suicide, leaving four broken-hearted children behind. The youngest child saw hope, and a light at the end of the tunnel. This youngest child feels his dad near, and finds peace. I remember once hearing that this youngest child had struggled with hearing loss, bipolar and too much drinking. But by getting through his problems, he learned how to comfort me. When tragedy strikes, sometimes the ones who have been through the wringer, survive the best.

Sometimes people say that I can't be trusted to say the right thing, do the right thing, think the right thing, or feel the right thing. This used to bother me, but now I try to be an independent thinker. It's true that I say, do, think, and feel the wrong things—at least what seems wrong to others and sometimes wrong to me. But that's how I learn. And I'm trying to be easy on myself—to love myself—after a lifetime of unhealthy guilt and undeserved shame. I have raw edges, but I'm not finished learning yet.

Recently, I testified in court against a serial rapist and murderer. I had to testify on behalf of a family member who was too traumatized to testify. Additional family members have also had their boundaries violated against their will by the foolish, disrespect of others. The scars last for a lifetime. It seems they reside in the cells of the body. Even though I no longer feel guilt most of the time, I have to fight a general sense of fear and shame every day when I wake up. I am victorious. I win my battles to regain self-respect each new day. It is a lifelong war. To survive something as destructive and soul-searing as sexual abuse, affects one's sense of self and safety so deeply.

Love. Intimacy. Family. Happiness. These things are worth fighting for at whatever the cost—either to be healed or to be protected.

An Autumn Diary 2018

I enjoy being near Butterfly's family in Kentucky. They have fun in spite of their family's challenges and traumas. They have foot paintings on their walls; they blow up pumpkins loaded with explosives in their backyard shooting range; and they dye their pet bunnies pink and blue.

Down the road from Butterfly's house, I also have fun—I put on performances in a hospital with my guitar, singing everything from "Supercalifragilisticexpialidocious," to Greg's and my original love songs such as "There Was Once Upon a Time I was Your Girlfriend."

Before my first performance, one of the hospital employees told me he knew who I was. To my surprise, he named one of the songs I wrote and told me I was famous. I was so confused. "I'm not famous," I said. Then he told me he saw my name on the activities calendar at the hospital and looked me up on YouTube and saw me sing my song, "Forever Loving You." I smile over the memory of recording that song, and over the memory of my hospital performance that day. I love to connect with people and share my heart through music.

I continue to get frazzled and upset easily. Yet, simple things uplift me—like a stranger I passed on the street while I was upset about being lost in a new city. She was wearing a shirt that said "Be more cool." A smile lit up my face as I told her how much I loved her shirt, and instantly, my cares dissolved.

Life can still be a Roller Coaster. Yet, no matter what life brings, my dream is to leave behind uplift and love—after all I've gone through.

AFTERWARD

By Beverly Ann Needham
January 24, 2019

Someone told me in the early 90's, that things would get easier with time. Things got worse before they got better. However, since the Spring of 1999, I've had an upper hand on mental illness. And writing continues to help me process what's happening in my life.

In 1999, I completed the first draft of this book "If You Are Struggling," and found healing for my split personality from trauma therapist Patrick Poor. Immediately after my healing, I wrote 7 new book drafts and recorded dozens of original songs. Not long after, a family friend, Milo Osmun—who had observed me as I went through my 13 years of depression—watched me as I emerged out of mental illness. He read manuscripts I wrote and he listened to songs I composed, and said, "Your healing unleashed a reservoir of creativity."

Writing continues to be my best medicine. Sometimes I write 100 pages in one day. I've dragged heavy trash bags full of diaries to the dumpster—after taking out the parts I want to keep. Sometimes I burn my diaries after removing valuable memories.

The other day, I enjoyed writing about Bonfires in my diary, as follows.

"I start my story with a bonfire. It's the kind you sit in front of with friends on a starry night when you leave the city to go camping in the mountains.

You hear the crackle of logs popping. The fiery glow of red, orange and yellow takes your breath away in upward bursts of explosive heat.

The cold air chills your back but you move back further into the cold, because your face is too hot near the flames. And when the embers die down to white coals, you go to bed in your sleeping bag, feeling as if you are in a different world. And you feel as if you are a different person."

After my life experiences, I am a different person, and I hope you will be too, after reading my story. Thank you for sharing my heart with me.

I recorded songs to go along with my writings, and placed some of them on You Tube. It gives me joy to think that I might help someone who is struggling. (See Beverly Ann Needham, You Tube.)

APPENDIX 1

Poetic Life Sketch

A SUMMARY OF MY LIFE
    Dear friend, I'd like to tell you
    About this life I've weathered.
    But first I'll make a time line
    To pull it all together:

7/22/53–1965
    I was born near L. A.,
    In nineteen fifty-three.
    Multiple personality
    Began when I was three.

    A youth with song and travel,
    And pets, and friends, and fun,
    Piano lessons, good grades,
    And two guitars to strum.

    I valued all my friendships,
    Which I held to faithfully.
    A grade school trauma tore me up—
    My second 'split' personality.

1965-1974

Four 'splits' emerged when I was 12:
Mistrust, and fear of men,
Shame, and guilt, and feeling 'bad',
I disowned myself, again.

I had religion taught to me.
It was my guiding light.
Although filled with confusion,
I tried to choose the right.

Then I met my best friend,
And the Burk family.
They were fun and musical,
And life grew sweet for me.

At age sixteen I dated.
I fell in love and grew
A split to compensate
For confusion which I knew.

My outside self was happy,
Unless the splits came out.
I managed to avoid them,
And I took a cheerful route.

The splits that made me hate men,
And fear, and feel ashamed,
Stayed mostly hidden in my mind,
So I could play life's 'game'.

4/23/74-1986
> Then marriage came, and family.
> The times were mostly glad.
> But sometimes 'splits' would make me feel
> Very, very sad.
>
> All the pain from all the years
> Had just been laying low,
> Waiting for a chance to heal.
> And 'splits' began to blow.

10/86-11/95
> I had a breakdown of my pride,
> My hidden pain came out.
> Doctors gave me medicine,
> They tried to help, no doubt.
>
> But my depression just got worse,
> In spite of all their care.
> I couldn't overcome my foes.
> My heart fought with despair.

11/95-2/99
> My doctor saw, at last, the foe,
> But he didn't have a cure—
> Multiple personalities
> Were what I faced for sure.
>
> More medication, and more prayer,
> More hope and faith and love.
> A miracle that I survived
> The traumas I knew of.

In desperation, fearing death,
From suicide, for sure,
I sought a humble intern.
In hopes he had a cure!

2/99-3/99

Intern Pat Poor showed me how
To release all my pain
Kept inside from all those years
Where my hopes seemed in vain.

3/99-2019

The violence and suicide
That tempted me so long
Finally found a solid cure,
A cure that still goes on.

When I learned with love and trust
To let past traumas heal,
I was free to learn from life,
And use my own free will.

Free from suicide and rage,
From old pain, and from hate,
I face my problems with a mind
Which tires, but does not break.

APPENDIX 2

Factual Life Sketch

A FEW MAIN EVENTS IN MY LIFE
BY BEVERLY ANN NEEDHAM

7/22/53
I was born in Southern California, in a city called La Mesa. As a child I liked school, animals, singing, writing, and playing with my five brothers and sisters. As a teen I liked friends, playing the guitar and the piano, and camping.

4/19/74
I graduated with a Bachelor's degree from Brigham Young University with a teaching credential for elementary school.

4/23/74
I married Greg Needham and taught elementary school for three years.

6/23/77-10/21/84
Greg and I had our first six children. Greg worked as an engineer and I worked in the home taking care of our family. Enjoying kids, we hiked, gardened, read lots of stories, camped, made bread from scratch, and did a lot of playing.

10/1986-1999

I came down with mental illness. It was diagnosed as 'clinical depression'. I continuously took psychiatric medicines until 1999. I performed a bit musically in hometown stage productions with some of my children. I traveled coast to coast across North America with seven children camping. I had my last baby in 1992. At the same time some of my teens were getting into drug abuse. We participated in a wilderness rehabilitation program, (Anasazi), for one of them. I home taught a few of my children. I volunteered service in the community and in local schools and in churches in my spare time. Each summer my family took in foreign exchange students from Japan, Indonesia, Spain, Taiwan, Australia, Germany, France, Austria, Russia, and Finland. We also took in two homeless teenagers. I saw one of my children recover from drug addiction. At the same time, I struggled with my own mental problems, landing in a psychiatric hospital for a few weeks.

2/99-3/99

I found a cure for multiple personality disorder, through the therapist Patrick Poor, of Riverside, California, using "Trauma Conversion Therapy."

3/99-2019

I have been writing, composing songs, recording music, traveling, and enjoying my family and additional foreign exchange students from China and Denmark. I continue to struggle to face my mental weaknesses compassionately. I take no medication because medication tends to make me suicidal and violent, and takes the edge off of my self-control. I've continued learning how to heal past and present traumas, and I've begun putting some of my songs on YouTube. It gives me joy to think that what I've gone through may help other people.

APPENDIX 3

Songs to Share

My 1999 healing unleashed a reservoir of creativity; I wrote several more books which have yet to be published, and recorded nearly a hundred songs to share with my books. Some of my songs may be found on YouTube under "Beverly Ann Needham".

Songs to Share

Writing pours my soul out,
My heart lives in my song.
I love to write. I love to sing.
In song my dreams go on.

I tell of holding onto faith,
When pain is everywhere.
I bear my heart to wounded souls,
My faith and hope to share.

For we live in a crazy world,
It's hard to get along.
Validation lifts us,
When pain drags on and on.

In book and song, a story,
Of love that never ends.
I hope to ease your loneliness,
And give you hope, my friend.

Always a Dream

Melody and Lyrics-Beverly Ann Needham (written 2000)

Verse One
>Have you ever had a dream in your heart,
>A dream that will not go away?
>Have you waited for a lifetime to see its flight begin,
>While the skies were heavy and gray?

Verse Two
>I will give my heart to dreams revived although they once were dead,
>With all of my strength I will give.
>I have barely gained ground but my dreams still shine bright.
>They give me a reason to live.

Chorus
>My dreams soar to the highest mountain,
>And far 'cross the dark stormy sea.
>My dreams sail like eagles with flight unrestrained,
>You can't take my dreams from me.

Verse Three
>I don't see the answers, nor the strength.
>It's hard to find my way.
>I only have faith for a start.
>But if I am patient with my dreams,
>I know they will come true.
>I feel it inside of my heart.

(Repeat Chorus.)

I'll Love You As You Are

Lyrics-Beverly Ann Needham (written 2000)
Melody-John Cameron and K. Newell Dayley's "Every Star is Different", © Kanada 1980, used by permission.

Verse One
    If your mind has splintered,
    And pain won't go away,
    A friend, a prayer, a kindness,
    Might help you through the day.
    Thoughts of something happy,
    Might help you through the night.
    Faith to keep on trying,
    Might help you hold on tight.

Chorus
    Child, you are young, and you are lonely.
    I'll sing to you my song, and love you kindly.
    I'll take you as you are. I will wait for you.
    I will not give up. I'll see you through.

Verse Two
    Hang on tight. Don't give up,
    When faith is hard to find.
    Let my hope in your good heart
    Calm your troubled mind.
    Love and safety wait beyond
    Your trouble and your grief.
    Ride on hopes and dreams and prayers
    Until you find relief.

I'll Never Forget You

Lyrics-Beverly Ann Needham (written in memory of Uncle Doug's compassion extended to me upon my release from the psychiatric hospital in 1995)

Melody-John Cameron and K. Newell Dayley's "Every Star is Different", © Kanada 1980, used by permission.

Verse One
> When the storm is raging,
> With no anchor in sight,
> When you fear you'll crash before
> You see the morning light.
> A friend who does not judge you
> But loves you as you are
> Is all you need to make it,
> No matter where you are.

Chorus
> Hear my prayer.
> Is someone there?
> I need someone to share.
> Too much pain to bear.
> Is somebody there, to share my lonely prayer?
> I need someone to share, someone to care.

Verse Two
> Thank you for your friendship.
> Thank you for your love.
> You lift up my sad heart.
> I see the sun above.
> You have given me hope.
> I'll never forget you.
> The memory of your kindness
> Touches all I do.

My Inspiration

Lyrics and Melody-Beverly Ann Needham (written 1/16/96 to my husband for our twenty-five year anniversary for having met)

Verse One
> When I'm alone, and feeling sad,
> I long for your kind touch so bad.
> I need you near to calm life's storms.
> For in your arms my strength is born.

Verse Two
> I love the way you make me feel,
> The warm glow remains here still.
> And when you're far, I keep a trace
> Of you upon my smiling face.

Verse Three
> Your sweet love makes my heart sigh.
> Your smile for me can make me fly.
> The memory that you leave me
> Calms my heart and sets it free.

Chorus
> Thank you for your goodness and love.
> You're the one I'm dreaming of.
> You're so sweet, you're tender and kind.
> I'm blessed because forever you're mine.

APPENDIX 4

Questions for Book Clubs and Study Groups

1. Why do you think Beverly desired mental health?

2. Why do you think Beverly didn't just give up?

3. What benefits come—when we are struggling—from thinking of the good times?

4. What are some ways that Beverly protected herself from acting out violent and suicidal thoughts?

5. What meaningful things occurred in Beverly's life during the years that she was mentally ill?

6. What things did Beverly do to cope with her mental challenges? What other things might she have done?

7. Where did Beverly turn for help when life wasn't going the way she had hoped it would?

8. What activities did Beverly engage in that strengthened her mental health?

9. How did Beverly cope with changes in her life, and how can others cope with changes in their own lives?

10. What made Beverly lose some of her mental health battles which she fought?

BOOK REFERENCES

"Men Are From Mars and Women Are From Venus" by Dr. John Gray

"The Path to Wholeness" by Carol Tuttle, © 1993 Carol Tuttle, Library of Congress Catalog Card No. 93-071760, Covenant Communications, Inc.

"The Velveteen Rabbit"

"Eliminate Your S D B's* (*Self-Defeating Behaviors)" by Jonathan M. Chamberlain, © 1978 Brigham Young University Press, Provo, UT 84602 (Fourth Printing 1980)

"Getting to Know the Real You" by Sterling G. & Richard G. Ellsworth, Deseret Book Company

"Fascinating Womanhood" by Helen B. Andelin

Beverly Ann Needham graduated with a bachelor's degree from Brigham Young University, taught elementary school, and married her rocket scientist husband Gregory A. Needham who graduated from UC Davis with a PhD in physics. Together they raised seven children. A writer, musician, teacher, and philanthropist, Beverly shares her life experiences with humility and frankness. She treats the subject of mental illness with compassion and understanding, for she spent many years suffering from depression, bipolar disorder, and multiple personality disorder. Her audience is primarily those who are struggling.

Royalties I pray shall go
To help the poor and weary,
Revive lost dreams, restore dead hopes,
Where prospects may seem dreary.
B. A. N.

Soon to be released in 2019

A Reason to Live
a novel
By Beverly Ann Needham

A Reason to Live is a true story about Sam, an autistic man who saves countless lives, breaks countless windows and is addicted to Crystal Meth.

Sam's uncanny awareness of his surroundings and his ability to live in the moment plunges him into saving lives in places where the police and firemen dare not go. On the other hand, when something frustrates him, his quick reflexes lead him to shatter the nearest window without thinking until it is too late.

www.ingramcontent.com/pod-product-compliance
Lightning Source LLC
Chambersburg PA
CBHW030112100526
44591CB00009B/381